British Design & Art Direction
in collaboration with Rotovision SA
and Shots – The Creative Video Programme

The Commercials Book

ROTOVISION

Acknowledgments

Cover and Book Design
Fernando Gutiérrez

Art Direction
Mike Dempsey

Cover Photograph
Oliviero Toscani
for COLORS Magazine #16: A Town

Design
Peartree Design Associates

Editors
Peter Ettedgui
Paul Kemp Robertson

Project Manager
Marcelle Johnson

Project Co-ordinator
John Green

With special thanks to

FrameStore for their sponsorship of
The Commercials Book

Shots – The Creative Video Programme
for their support and for producing the
accompanying showreel

DUBBS for supporting the production of
The Commercials Book

D&AD would also like to thank all the
directors who so generously gave their
time for this book.

Published by Rotovision SA
7 rue du Bugnon
CH-1299 Crans
Switzerland
Tel: +41 22776 0511
Fax: +41 22776 0889

Rotovision Sales and Production Office
Sheridan House
112-116A Western Road
Hove BN3 2AA
UK
Tel: +44 1273 7272 68
Fax: +44 1273 7272 69

First published 1997
Copyright © British Design & Art Direction 1997
A D&AD Mastercraft series publication

Production and Separation in Singapore by ProVision Pte Ltd
Tel: +65 334 7720
Fax: +65 334 7721

Printed in Singapore

ISBN No 2-88046-341-9

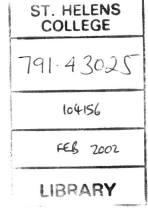

FrameStore

To become a film director takes single-mindedness and vision. To become a master of the craft of commercial making also requires that most elusive of qualities – originality.

You have probably wondered, like me, how on earth they pull it off so consistently. In these pages you will be given some insight into the techniques that have made them masters of creative vision and craft skills.

You will enjoy being reminded of the highlights from the portfolios of these 31 directors who have formed and influenced the craft of commercial film making and I hope you will find it inspiring, as I have.

This volume celebrates original voices among the packets of soap powder, go-faster cars and pairs of jeans. FrameStore is delighted to be associated with D&AD's celebration of excellence.

Sharon Reed

FrameStore

Contents

6
8
10
16
22
28
34
40
46
52
58
64
70
76
82
88
94
100
106
112
116
122
128
134
140
146
152
158
164
170

Preface

Foreword

Aardman Animations

Daniel Barber

Michael Bay

Bob Brooks

Frank Budgen

John S. Clarke

Jonathan Glazer

Michel Gondry

Jean-Paul Goude

Jerry Hibbert

Hugh Hudson

Daniel Kleinman

Ian McMillan

Andy Morahan

Barry Myers

Louis Ng

Mehdi Norowzian

Ridley Scott

Joe Sedelmaier

Michael Seresin

Peter Smillie

Tarsem

João Daniel Tikhomiroff

Kinka Usher

Vaughan Arnell & Anthea Benton

Paul Weiland

Roger Woodburn

Howard Zieff

**Preface by
Anthony Simonds-Gooding
Chairman, D&AD**

The commercials medium is one of the most significant developments in the film and television industries over the last thirty years. It has irrevocably altered the language of the moving image, while offering film-makers the world over an opportunity to practise their craft and develop their sensibility. When the indigenous film industry in the UK has gone into one of its frequent periods of decline, commercials have proved a mainstay for the directors and technicians who work within it.

As the team from Aardman Animations point out in this book, had it not been for the patronage of the advertising industry, Wallace and Gromit might never have had the opportunity to become the phenomenon they are.

In the pages that follow, you will meet directors with agency backgrounds for whom advertising is a vocation; directors whose first loyalty is to the film medium rather than the client and product; directors who represent traditional film-making values and directors who personify the shock of the new. Some readers may point to those notable by their absence. In a book of this size we could not hope to feature all the greats – aside from other factors, their punishing schedules and, in some cases, natural self-effacement have influenced the final line-up. But what binds all these contributors together is the importance they place on narrative. Even the more experimental and visually-inclined directors acknowledge how essential it is to put the highly sophisticated

tools of their trade to the service of telling a story and creating believable characters. Our contributors also share a high degree of perfectionism, tempered by the knowledge that their medium is the most unpredictable and volatile of all art forms. As Orson Welles once put it, "a director is one who presides over accidents."

While these contributions are peppered with tricks of the trade and tips about working practices, perhaps the best lesson these directors collectively offer is that there is no magic formula for making a good commercial. Ultimately, it's the contributors' individual creativity that makes them successful film-makers. The way this book has come together was greatly influenced by that creativity. We wanted each

director who appears in the following pages to be able to decide on the specific content of their chapters themselves. Some chose to feature more examples of their work than others; some chose to present storyboards or design sketches as well as frames from their commercials; some wanted to include examples of work from media other than advertising – pop promos, or short films, for example.

The basis for the text in each chapter was a series of interviews conducted by our editors. Although the edited material was then polished by the contributors, it is hoped something of the informality and conversational style in which they articulated their thoughts survives in the book.

As well as thanking them for giving us such invaluable and inspiring insights into their work, I would also like to thank our designer, Fernando Gutiérrez, editors Peter Ettedgui and Paul Kemp Robertson and Shots – The Creative Video Programme for producing the showreel which accompanies this book. Lastly, I would also add my personal thanks to FrameStore for sponsoring this, the third title in D&AD's Mastercraft series.

Anthony Simonds-Gooding
Chairman, D&AD

When I started my career in advertising in 1958, the components of an ad were really very simple, unsophisticated even – a product, a logo, a price, a stockist and a claim. Invariably, the claim was that the product was either 'new' or 'improved' or sometimes 'new and improved'. It was what might best be described as a 'customer ad', aimed at offering a product for sale which the public would probably at some point want: you might buy Dunlop instead of Avon, but one way or another you needed a new tyre.

By 1965 all that had changed. Ads began to set out to convince human beings that their 'lifestyle' required certain products which they'd possibly never heard of, let alone thought about, and that, for the most part, they almost certainly didn't need. It amounted to what I'd now term 'consumer advertising', and it involved a completely different approach. It was largely made possible by that remarkable mood of confidence and optimism which, in the early sixties, would spawn some quite extraordinary talents in the commercials world.

These changes revolutionised Britain's potential for creative and innovative advertising. It encouraged the demand for a new breed of image-makers, people who were prepared to experiment with all kinds of visual ideas drawn from an astonishingly eclectic range of sources. At the same time,

the rise of commercial television in Britain, in the form of the fledgling ITV network provided opportunities for working with moving images as well as the conventional static forms. It was this mood of change which created early opportunities for some of the people featured in this book, and laid the ground for successive generations of commercials directors for the next 30 years.

What quickly became apparent was the emergence of an ever-increasing cross-fertilisation of ideas among different disciplines, particularly between the worlds of advertising, film, fashion and design. In the early 1960s I joined Collett Dickenson Pearce. At CDP I was among a group working with Charles Saatchi, Alan Parker and Ridley Scott – all in all, a pretty remarkable team. In between hours spent practising tap-dancing, we'd work out an award-winning ad. It was a fantastic time. We'd be screaming with laughter, and generally horsing about, meanwhile creating some quite memorable work which sometimes even sold the product!

But I'd long had ambitions to launch into the movies and it wasn't long before Cramer Puttnam Saatchi was formed with two ex-colleagues from CDP and we unveiled plans to start making films. "We're going to go into the movie industry," we told an astonished Alan Parker. "Don't be stupid!"

was his thoughtful response. When we suggested that he might like to write a couple of scripts for us, he pointed out that he'd never written anything much more than 30 seconds long. But our enthusiasm and passionate belief in Alan's talent knew no bounds. In any case, we already had another project which Charles Saatchi had written called 'Carpet Man' based on a Jimmy Webb song which we believed could be turned into a successful vehicle for Gene Wilder.

After an early fund-raising trip to New York ended in disaster, Charles sensibly announced that he'd had enough of the movies and was going off to open an advertising agency. Suddenly, it looked as if Alan was right, we were crazy to even consider trading the secure and highly-paid world of 30-second TV commercials for the risk-laden and unknown world of feature film production.

But I persevered and Alan eventually wrote a script for £500 about a love affair between school kids in a South London comprehensive. It was from that script that 'Melody' was born, and cheques from the film helped keep me and my partner Sandy Lieberson going for a long time afterwards.

Other people tentatively followed and ever since there's been a constant cross-fertilisation between commercials and the movies. As Hugh Hudson observes, at the beginning of the 1970s

those making commercials were constantly borrowing ideas and styles from feature films. At the time commercials often took the form of short stories compressed into a minute or even less. The ability to put anything worthwhile across in that timeframe requires a rigour, a discipline and a skill which in many ways provides an ideal training ground for working in the longer medium.

As the biographical sketches in the following pages demonstrate, most commercials directors tend to emerge from a visual background, having studied painting or photography at art college. In this respect they have a singular advantage over many of their counterparts in television who tend to emerge from a literary or theatrical background and are therefore far more used to working with words than images. As a consequence, when commercials directors make the transition to the movies, the resulting work is often significantly more cinematic than that of TV directors who tend to remain overly fond of dialogue and the type of literary conceits which can end up hindering the visual development of the story.

Many commercials directors also have the advantage of shooting a huge amount of footage every year, and spend a great deal of their time looking through the lens of a camera. That gives them a freedom to experiment – a freedom to fail even – that is utterly invaluable.

Commercials directors, just like their counterparts in feature film, deal in a kind of heightened reality, a world comprised of artificial and deliberately attractive images. Both are in the seduction business. Both are looking to create visual images that steal up on you quietly, subtly winning you over, shifting your attitudes and working away at your emotions.

Yet for years, many of us coming out of advertising experienced a form of crude snobbery from among certain more traditional elements of the British film industry. In their eyes, a background in commercials was somehow evidence of an impurity, something quite distinct from the creation of real cinema – whatever that might be. To the contrary, it's always seemed to me that our background equipped us especially well for working in the movies, and not only because of our awareness of the importance of reaching an audience.

Like cinema, the best commercials beguile, inspire and entertain. Creating something that has genuine mass appeal is, after all, an ambition that at its best goes well beyond a crude preoccupation with the lowest common denominator. Commercials may not be the best possible medium for putting across complex ideas, but they can be unbelievably successful at creating a series of powerful, lasting images which linger in the viewer's mind long after many others have faded.

British commercials directors, designers and advertising copywriters are among the very best. They have had a significant influence on their peers all over the world. But whatever their nationality, and wherever they are working, commercials directors are a crucial element in what might now be called 'industries of the creative imagination'. Poised, as we are, on the threshold of a global information economy, that seems a genuinely desirable place to be. It's clear too that these skills will have an increasingly critical part to play in shaping the economies of the new millennium.

Like it or not we live in an age in which moving images pervade every aspect of our lives. Advertising is at the heart of all of this. Strong visual marketing is increasingly vital to the success of any company or product – however great its intrinsic merits may be. We're constantly being asked to buy into the images, whether it be a political party or a new brand of lemonade. This timely and fascinating book is a testament to the skills, inventiveness and sheer dedication of those who create these images, and give them an ever-increasing importance in the fabric of our everyday lives.

Sir David Puttnam CBE

Photo: Terence Donovan

In 1976, Peter Lord and David Sproxton began making films as Aardman Animations. Specialising in clay animation, they worked on children's series such as 'Take Hart', creating the character Morph and short films commissioned by Channel 4 and BBC2. Their success attracted the attention of advertising agencies and they began to produce commercials and pop videos. Nick Park joined the thriving partnership in 1985 as director and animator, bringing with him Wallace and Gromit, the stars of 'A Grand Day Out', the short film he started while studying at the National Film and Television School. The phenomenal success of these characters has helped to make Aardman a household name, and added Oscar® and BAFTA recognition to the animation and advertising awards garnered internationally by the company for its work.

All three of us began making films with plasticine and super-8 cameras as a hobby when we were kids. The great thing about our earliest kitchen table experiments was the element of surprise. You'd spend a week making your film frame by frame, send it off to the labs, and only really know what you'd done a few days later when the developed film was returned. The thrill of seeing your labours come to life for the first time was unbeatable – a feeling it's hard to reproduce in the video assist era. The big advantage of starting young is that you have no inhibitions. You just do what comes naturally. People who begin animating in art school are often intimidated by the technical demands of the medium.

We were lucky when we started out because our style and technique were unknown on British TV. We were literally the only people in the world, as far as we knew, who were animating with plasticine. So, even if you did the simplest and most obvious things, such as animating a lump of plasticine to squodge around like some primitive life-form, it was easy to make an impact when no one else was using the medium.

The great thing about plasticine is that it gives you absolute control. Sure it's an awkward material to work with – slow and dirty – but if you've got the time and patience, you can always make it look exactly the way you want. A good analogy is the pencil. It's simple to use, costs 60p, and is incredibly subtle. You can draw the finest grain line, or a great

fat dark one, and just with the pressure of your hand, make it express anything. Likewise plasticine – you can change the mass, model it to catch, say, the exact slump of the shoulders in a character who's depressed. It's incredibly expressive. Also, because it's so malleable, you can be spontaneous in front of camera and make adjustments right up to the last second before you shoot.

We don't have a house style so much as a house ethos. We all share an enormous love for the medium, and also an extreme perfectionism. A lot of what we do is based on observation. We don't do extravagant Tex Avery-style animation, but we'll spend a lot of time doing characters scratching their ear. Working on series like 'Conversation Pieces' and 'Creature Comforts', we learned a huge amount just listening to the voices recorded for us to animate with. You'd hear how someone's attention wanders as they speak, how their train of thought is broken, how often there are amazing gaps in their speech. You might pick up on that with a change in the eye-line or a little glance away, or show that the character is nervous by twitching their fingers. So an awkward silence can become quite rich. A great thing about animation is that audiences know that every tiny detail is hand-crafted, that nothing happens by chance or accident. This helps us enormously because it means that people are that much more attuned to picking up detail than they might be when they watch live action.

Drawing and doodling are very important to us. There can be great energy in a well-executed doodle which gives you the basis for a character. It quite often happens that you're sitting in a pre-production meeting hitting your head against a brick wall with a problem. You start doodling, spin the pad round – and there's the answer in a convincing drawing. Students on the course we run here do life drawing. It's so important for the way it makes you think about the human body. Of course, if you can't draw well, it doesn't mean you can't animate or direct well, but it does impair your ability to get an idea across effectively when you come to storyboarding. We were all brought up on comics like *The Beano* and *Dandy* – cartoon strips which were very filmic, much like storyboards; so storyboarding is second nature to us. But it's also the key to directing in animation, because it's the best way of communicating information, conveying ideas in shorthand and expressing them very directly and succinctly. When you're shooting, you may well have six different animators at some stage animating your hero, so imposing a style is crucial. If you've got cartooning ability, you can make the storyboard express the kind of performance you want. This is vital – because you don't have several takes to get a performance right.

Directing puppet/model animation is very much like live action. You have a very similar relationship with your DOP, your set designers and model-makers. Instead of actors, you've got anima-

tors. You'll go through the action and motivation of the characters with them. You may act out the performance for them, then get them to perform it back for you to make sure they've understood. If you want a character to jump out of a chair, there's no substitute for doing the action yourself, feeling where the weight goes, how the limbs and joints articulate. You have to collaborate to get the best out of creative people; the trick is to sort out the ideas that are better than yours from the ones that are worse.

There's a natural partnership between our work in commercials and the short films we make. Making successful short films has given Aardman an identity and made it possible for us to make successful TV commercials. That in turn has made us sufficiently financially independent to keep the short films coming. In fact, we try not to make great distinctions between the two worlds. We reckon it's all film-making. Making commercials makes you much sharper as a director – because you have to learn to tell a story in an incredibly concise form. It's a tough discipline: an ability which feeds back into everything else you do. Conversely, giving our animators the opportunity to make their own films not only re-energises them but makes them better film-makers. They bring back to commercials the knowledge they've acquired while tackling their own stories and making them work. It also, incidentally, gives them a showcase for their talent which can sometimes spark with an agency hungry for new ideas.

Temperamentally, we all tend to be perfectionist and very craft-based – maybe most animators do. Ours is still a very traditional way of making films – it's extremely hands-on. We see no need to change the core skills we have, though it makes sense to add to them. People always ask about computer animation and whether it will replace our current methods. Why should it? Why should you replace something that is so simple and works so well? We'd rather look on computer animation as an addition to our basic skills – another way of making animation – rather than a replacement. It's another tool for expression and performance, and that's what we'll use it for! We reckon that we have the best plasticine animators – many that we've trained in-house – but we always continue to introduce new ideas, new styles, new ways of film-making. Young directors who have joined us recently like Luis Cook or Sam Fell contribute new energy and new techniques to the mix.

The advertising industry has become an essential mainstay for animation in the UK. Not only has it kept so many animators employed and able to practise their craft, but it's also enabled us to work with much higher production values. Were it not for commercials, we would never have been able to invest so much time and money in 'The Wrong Trousers'. Contrary to what people may think, Wallace and Gromit wasn't a commercial venture at all. We were going out on a long limb – and that was made possible by our work in advertising.

Aardman Animations

Asleep
Butter
Butter
Cheese Spread
Christmas
Obedient
Love Story

Frank the Tortoise
Pablo
Carol the Cat
Orang-utans
Pandas
Penguins
Pigs

Lurpak Campaign
1993
Douglas constantly tries to interrupt the commercial to play his trombone. Mixture of live action and animation.

Total Heating Campaign
1996
Award-winning campaign based on Nick Park's Oscar winner 'Creature Comforts'.

Directors
Peter Lord
Steve Box
David Sproxton

Producers
Julie Lockhart
Carla Shelley

Copywriter
Nick Gill

Art Director
Tony Davidson

Animators
Peter Lord
Steve Box
Peter Peake

Lighting Camera
Steve Downer, Mike Garfath (Live Action)
David Sproxton (Animation)

Set Design
Peter Lord
Tim Farrington

Production Company
Aardman Animations

Post Production
The Mill
VTR
Soho 601

Agency
BMP DDB Needham

Agency Producers
Howard Spivey
Sarah Pollitt

Client
MD Foods

Directors
Nick Park
Peter Lord

Producer
Chris Moll

Creative Director
Paul Cardwell

Animators
Nick Park
Peter Lord

Lighting Camera
David Sproxton
Tristan Oliver
Dave Alex Riddett

Set Design
Michael Wright
Jonathan Leigh
Tim Farrington
Stuart Rose

Production Company
Aardman Animations

Post Production
SVC

Agency
GGK

Agency Producer
Joanne Cresser

Client
Electricity Board

Classic
Classic
Cool
Cool
Corridor
Corridor
Scales

Hoots Mon

Polo Campaign
1995
Campaign to promote four different brands of Polo, all within one working factory.

Maynard's Wine Gums 'Hoots Mon'
1993
A commercial for Maynard's Wine Gums using a mixture of live action and animation and a difference matting post production technique. Not at all Scottish-ist!

Directors
Luis Cook
Peter Lord

Producer
Julie Lockhart

Copywriter
Nick Wootton

Art Director
Jonathan John

Animators
Luis Cook
Will Byles

Lighting Camera: 'Classic'
Frank Passingham

Lighting Camera: 'Cool', 'Corridor'
Tristan Oliver

Lighting Camera: 'Scales'
Mark Chamberlain

Design
Luis Cook
Rachel Moore
Mark Brierly

Composer
Pete Brandt

Production Company
Aardman Animations

Post Production
VTR

Agency
J. Walter Thompson

Agency Producer
Jenny Carty

Client
Nestlé Rowntree

Directors
David Sproxton
Dave Alex Riddett

Producer
Clare Thalmann

Copywriter
Pete Lewtas

Art Director
Jonathon Prime

Animators
Fred Reed
Dave Alex Riddett

Lighting Camera
Tom McDougal

Design
David Butt

Production Company
Aardman Animations

Post Production
Rushes

Agency
BMP DDB Needham

Agency Producer
Michael Parker

Client
Trebor Bassett Ltd

Terrence Higgins Trust 'Nobs in Space'
1994
An intergalactic spaceship discovers the benefits of wearing a condom. Very low budget production. Parody of a parody of Flash Gordon. Most difficult technique – making the strings that hold up planets show up!

Walkers Snack Shack 'L'Arrival'
1997
Quentin Quaverhead and the Monster Munch Bunch meet their new noisy neighbours. Many logistical problems occurred when incorporating three different products and designs under one banner.

Directors
Dave Alex Riddett
Luis Cook

Producer
Jo Allen

Copywriter
Tony Malcom

Art Director
Guy Moore

Animators
Dave Riddett
Luis Cook
Nick Upton

Lighting Camera
Dave Alex Riddett

Music
Amber Music

Production Company
Aardman Animations

Post Production
VTR

Agency
Simons Palmer Clemmow Johnson

Agency Producer
Jo Sayer

Client
Terrence Higgins Trust

Director
Dave Alex Riddett

Producer
Julie Lockhart

Copywriter
Dave Buchanan

Art Director
Mike Hannet

Animators
Dave Osmand
Sam Fell

Lighting Camera
Dave Alex Riddett
Paul Smith

Design
Michael Salter
Oliver Reid
Paul Smith

Music
Amber Music

Production Company
Aardman Animations

Post Production
Soho 601

Agency
BMP DDB Needham

Agency Producer
Anni Cullen

Client
Walkers

Weetabix 'Pirates'
1994
A re-write of the Marie Celeste tale which pays
homage to the style of legendary animator, George
Pal. Each head is individually sculpted in hard resin
with between 10-15 heads per character.

Director
Richard Goleszowski

Producer
Julie Lockhart

Copywriter
Gordon Graham

Art Director
Neil Sullivan

Animators
Richard Goleszowski
Chris Sadler
Tom Gasek

2D Animator
Mark Brierly

Lighting Camera
Frank Passingham

Designer
Rachel Moore

Music
Jo & Co

Production Company
Aardman Animations

Post Production
VTR

Agency
Lowe Howard-Spink

Agency Producer
Sue Braley

Client
Weetabix Limited

Bar

Daniel Barber was born in London on September 21st 1964. His first spoken word was 'car'. He learned to cycle before he was three. He learned to play the trumpet aged eight and was good at Lego by nine. He celebrated his Bar Mitzvah when he was 13. His best friend at school was Gary Peters, and he decided he loved girls at 14. Three years later he bought a EuroRail ticket. He started at St Martin's School of Art when he was 19 and met Sandra there. He graduated at 23. He married Sandra. He did things for telly at Lambie-Nairn. Then he joined Rose Hackney and shot loads of ads. His name went up above the door. He directed even more ads. Moses, his son, was born.

Commercials have really opened up a lot more to me. Everything I've done has depended on being given the right opportunities by the right people. Good creatives can make the leap about what you might be able to do for them or how you might be able to expand into different areas. I've been lucky enough to work on very diverse projects with lots of different agencies and products – and that's what makes this business so interesting.

As a director you go into a project commando-style: you just go absolutely mad and do everything you can to make it as good as you possibly can and then you're onto something completely different. This is really healthy – it means I have to think in different ways and it keeps my mind fresh, keeps me wanting to explore new and different things.

Agencies are doing more and more exciting things and advertising seems to talk down to the audience less now: clients are taking into account that audiences are far more visually advanced and receptive to extraordinary imagery. I came into commercials when Henry had just come on-line so I've grown up with that. I've never edited on film – I don't want to. I love Avid, I love Henry, I love all the latest cameras, the latest toys. Nothing fazes me technology-wise. I embrace it – I was born into the computer age and make the most of it.

My fine art background dictates the way I tackle commercials. I work in a very painterly way. I don't have a terribly strict or over-structured approach. I try to be relatively free-form in and around an idea, to find oddities and interesting things going on and that follows through to every-thing I do – to allow everybody as much freedom as possible. But I hold the reins so that the idea remains intact.

I look for a really good concept that affords me the opportunity to do something interesting visually with the script. If it doesn't really excite there is nowhere I can take it. As a 'visual' director to have a sense of freedom is very important. The best things I have done so far are where the agency has afforded me as much flexibility as possible on the backbone of their idea.

I like to have a loose notion of what I'm going to shoot. I prefer storyboards to hint at, rather than dictate, the area we'll be filming. This allows for fluidity and spontaneity.

Shooting is a double-edged sword for me. I have a very short amount of time to make definite decisions. When it's going well, shooting is the best thing in the world and when it's going badly you just want to hang yourself. I love all the different aspects of it – the thrill of receiving a fantastic script or when a meeting goes well.

I don't work in a vacuum, I work collaboratively. I'm not a musician, I'm not an art director and I'm not an editor – and I don't want to be. I want to be able to work with really talented people: they can all add so much more. My lighting cameraman and I are almost like a married couple – we share everything. I have to feel like that with the crew I work with – I'm not afraid to say to someone, "what do you think?", "what shall we do?".

What makes me successful? I'm like a bull terrier that will hang onto your ankles and will never let go – that's what I'll do with the script. I'll see the idea and however anyone wants to divert it or the art director wants to paint the set blue when it should be red or the cameraman wants to shoot in black and white when the whole thing must be in colour – I will always bring it back to what it needs to be.

I will give everyone as much freedom as possible but I have to rein them in. I'm good at it and I'm getting better at it. The more jobs I do the more confident I become.

I love beautiful and extraordinary images and I will go to ends of the earth to achieve them and I don't care about the money and I don't care about time. I just want to see the ultimate visually of what can be done.

I'm never happy with anything I do anyway and I don't think I ever will be to be honest. As soon as I finish a job I go into a slight depression and hope that the next one will make it better.

Why do painters paint and paint and paint and end up killing themselves?

Because they never do anything they genuinely love. They just keep going and keep trying and that's the way I work.

Daniel Barber

Per Second | Crash Test

Orange 'Per Second'
1995

I was given the opportunity by Rooney Carruthers and Larry Barker, the creative directors at WCRS, to work on the campaign for Orange, the mobile phone company. They afforded me great freedom in the development of three commercials. This one, my favourite, was based on the brief of time or cost per second of a telephone call. Filmed completely in a studio, I experimented with the idea of time. I filmed various time pieces and projected them into water, refilmed them and projected them onto people. In combination with some high-speed camera shots, the result is really quite unusual.

Daewoo 'Crash Test'
1995

"We want to crash some cars into a steel wall and then we want to have some people who run head first into the wall as well."

"Right!"

"Oh and by the way it's got to look really good and stylish."

"Ok!"

A great script as part of a great campaign that launched Daewoo in Britain – I would work for Duckworth Finn Grubb Waters anytime!

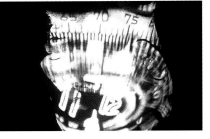 

Voice over

Orange think it unfair that you should pay for time you haven't used. And in the future maybe everyone will think that way. Until then Orange is the only mobile network to charge you one second at a time instead of rounding up to the next minute or half-minute.

The future's bright. The future's Orange.

Voice over

All car manufactures have to test their cars... Daewoo also believe it's by testing customers and dealing directly with them that we can analyse their problems with buying and owning cars and do something about it. Which is why we would like you to call us if you have ever run into problems with the motor trade. A car company that wants to hear complaints? That'll be the Daewoo.

Director
Daniel Barber

Producer
Karen Cunningham

Cameraman
Steve Chivers

Editor
Brian Dyke

Music
Philip Glass

Art Director
Rooney Carruthers

Copywriter
Larry Barker

Agency
WCRS

Director
Daniel Barber

Producer
Clare Mitchell

Cameraman
Ivan Bird

Editor
Duncan Shepherd

Music
Anthony & Gaynor Sadler

Art Director
Dave Waters

Copywriter
Paul Grubb

Agency
DFGW

BBC1 'Nine O'Clock News Ident'
1990

My first project on leaving college. I was very lucky to get a job with Lambie-Nairn and Company and one evening Martin Lambie-Nairn was working late trying to design a logo for the BBC 'Nine O'Clock News'. I asked him if he needed any help and on hearing "Yes please" I tried to design the title sequence. I had no idea how my initial sketches could be achieved technically, but through Martin's encouragement I was thrown into creating my vision. He sold my storyboard through the BBC and entrusted me with this rather large responsibility. At the time it caused a huge commotion, it really was different and as a title sequence for a news programme, it broke very new ground – anyway this was my 'baptism of fire'.

BBC1/BBC2 'Idents'
1992

Almost my second project at Lambie-Nairn & Co was to work with Martin on redesigning the on-screen identities for BBC1 and BBC2. I couldn't believe my luck, here I was 24 years old working alongside my hero of design on the pinnacle of any television graphic designer's career. I threw myself into it and the results are still on screen today. The two channels have very different personalities and quite diverse visual solutions: the numerous BBC2 logos arty and esoteric, hopefully always intriguing; and the richer, warmer, but in my view no less arty BBC1. In 1992 the on-screen identities for BBC2 were awarded a D&AD Silver Award and a BAFTA.

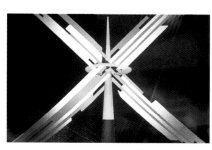

Director
Daniel Barber

Super-8 cameraman
Daniel Barber

Producer
Debbie Darby

Animation
Derek Hayes

Henry
Rob Harvey

Music
George Fenton

Designers/Directors
Daniel Barber/Martin Lambie-Nairn

Producer
Celia Chapman

Cameraman
Doug Foster

Model Makers
Asylum, Steve Wilshire

Henry
Rob Harvey

Music
Anthony & Gaynor Sadler

Daniel Barber

Armchair   Dreamboat

Sony Widescreen 'Armchair'
1995
'Wow' what a brief, a man falls in his armchair, from the sky and just as he is about to crash into a hangar on the ground, he changes channels on his TV to stop his hyper-real experience, only later to find his cat has also been caught up in the effect. Filmed for real in Los Angeles, with some of the best stuntmen in the world, a skydiving cameraman fell through the air to capture the images in my storyboard. I still can't believe we even attempted it.

BMW 'Dreamboat'
1996
I had done quite a few BMW ads in England for WCRS, when American agency Fallon McElligott asked me to work on this wonderful idea to launch the new '5' series.

American cars are known as boats: big ungainly wobbling things, so let's flood New York and show how lithe and efficient the new BMW is. So that's what we did: we flooded New York with 10 zillion gallons of spring water and drove the BMW around. Not quite, but that is what it looks like, thanks to a very precise special effects shoot in New York and Miami. Big thanks to Ivan Bird, Sean Broughton at Smoke & Mirrors and the fabulous Delano Hotel in Miami.

Director
Daniel Barber

Producer
Stephen Worley

Cameramen
Tom Sanders (aerial)
Ivan Bird

Editor
Duncan Shepherd

Music
Anthony & Gaynor Sadler

Art Director
Mike Bowles

Copywriter
Jerry Hollins

Agency
BMP DDB Needham

Director
Daniel Barber

Producer
Pete Christy

Cameraman
Ivan Bird

Editor
Duncan Shepherd

Art Director
Dean Hanson

Copywriter
Mike (two burgers) Lescarbo

Agency
Fallon McElligott, Minneapolis

Feet You Wear   **The Journey**

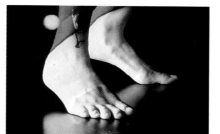

Adidas 'Feet You Wear'
1996
I wanted to work with Leagas Delaney for a long time, and here was my chance. Travel the world, shoot loads of athletes and combine them with feet to create something you have never seen before. A great brief and a series of ads I'm very pleased with. We shot feet in Los Angeles and athletes in Australia, America, Germany and France, came home and edited for a month in Flame at Smoke & Mirrors – thank you once again Sean.

Cointreau 'The Journey'
1997
One of my most recent ads, through BBH in London. A great script, with wonderful creatives who gave me loads of freedom in developing ideas and images about Cointreau being the longest drink in the world. Exhausting to make, but I did get a free bottle of Cointreau, which I have found is best drunk slammer-style very cold!

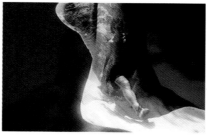

Director
Daniel Barber

Producer
Clare Mitchell

Cameraman
Stephen Blackman

Editor
Brian Dyke

Music
Propeller Head

Art Director
Warren Eakins

Copywriter
Tim Delaney

Agency
Leagas Delaney

Director
Daniel Barber

Producer
Carine Harris

Cameraman
Ivan Bird

Editor
Rick Russell

Art Director
Martin Galton

Copywriter
Dennis Lewis

Agency
Bartle Bogle Hegarty

Michael Bay

Bay

After receiving the Frank Capra Award for Best Student Film at America's Wesleyan University and a brief but successful stint doing pop promos, Michael Bay's first television commercial, for The American Red Cross, was honoured with a Gold at the Clio Awards. By the age of 26, Bay became one of the most sought-after commercials directors in the States, working on Nike, Budweiser, Levi's and Coca-Cola among others.

Working out of Propaganda Films, Bay's highly energised visual technique and strong wit ensured that in 1995 he became the youngest recipient of the Directors Guild of America 'Director of the Year' prize – the same year that his 'Aaron Burr' spot for Goodby Silverstein's popular Got Milk? campaign took the Grand Prix at the Clios. He has also won Gold and Silver Lions at Cannes for his work on Budweiser, Bugle Boy and Miller.

In 1995 Bay helmed the feature film 'Bad Boys', following up with 'The Rock' a year later. Combined, the two box office hits grossed more than $500 million worldwide. His third feature project is Disney's sci-fi thriller 'Armageddon', starring Bruce Willis.

What I look for in a script is something that challenges me, something that breaks new ground, something that allows me to flex my director muscle. You have got to think fast in this business, you've got to keep reinventing yourself to stay on top.

Having done two movies, I see commercials in a new light. There is so much bullshit and interference, so much red tape and the freedom of creativity is held back far too often. When you're the director of a movie, it's your movie yet on a commercial you're working for someone who can ultimately do whatever they want with your footage. There's still a lot of politics in movies, but creatively, they don't screw you up that much.

I think feature directors have a much harder time coming to commercials than the other way round. Advertising is so specific, you have to use and construct shots so differently. I like the economy of the format, the immediacy you get with fast cutting. Each second is precious, so you learn to

convey an amazing amount of information in a short space of time – which helped on my first movie, 'The Rock'.

Throughout my commercials career I have always been angling towards movies, trying to create movie-style scenarios. That was always my grand plan – and I was very open about it. At film school I sensed that advertising would be a great training ground. I wanted to do things that looked big. I wanted to do action, I wanted to do character stuff, I wanted to do comedy, I wanted to tell stories, I wanted to do cool images – anything to broaden my horizon. Compare being a commercials director with being a film director – you get so many more chances, you're at such an advantage if you're a young guy. I shot so many different scenarios and ran so many different crews – and all that made me so much more competitive.

I still feel loyal to commercials – and it bugs me when asshole movie critics say "oh, he's just a commercials director". I hate that kind of snobbery. Billy Wilder, one of the great American directors, said that he was always amazed how commercials directors can tell a story in 30 seconds – it's a real power.

I think it's dangerous though when some commercials directors are wooed by Hollywood studios before their time. It's best to serve an apprenticeship. I was offered movies for many years but I kept holding back, because I wanted to get really good at what I was doing.

I demand a lot of freedom. There was a time when I was really nervous about conference calls, but now I treat them like a piece of theatre. I really probe the creatives – I ask a lot of questions, suss their client out, see where they're all headed. I'd rather say no to a great script than be their prisoner.

Commercials are about commerce. You can soft-sell people, you can clever sell, you can make them laugh or you can just plain entertain them better than the last spot. It depends on the product,

but I generally go for the soft sell, I always try to do something entertaining, it's kinda always been my motto. My ads may be big but the product is not slammed in your face, it's woven into the story.

Being a commercials director, you're kind of like the boss and the slave all at once. The best part of my character is my incredible drive, my fear of failing. The psychological root behind this competitive streak is that I was an athlete when I was young and took sports really seriously. I look at directing as a sporting event. It's a race, a marathon. It's great when it clicks – which is why I push crews so hard so we can excel.

On set, I am not the demon some people make me out to be. I like cracking a good joke and I get a kick when people make fun of me – because at times I can be an asshole, though I never make a personal attack on someone. Crews know that they will have to work their asses off with me, but they know that we will all be proud of the end result. That's why the director's role is so important. We are

the guiding lights. The same crew could shoot another commercial and for whatever reason it could be totally lacklustre.

Out of all the weird things I've done in advertising, the stunts that stick out most in my mind are all for Budweiser – cutting through a 20ft wave on a reef in Fiji to get to my surf unit, getting stuck under an 18ft tiger shark in Hawaii – but my favourite has to be getting this 94 year-old woman to do push ups and call this guy a pussy!

It's great that I get accused of not being politically correct. People need to take themselves less seriously. The world is so screwed up as it is, we've all got to relax a bit more.

The perfect commercial is striking, it's witty, it sticks with you, it comes up in conversation and enters the pop culture. A perfect commercial is one that makes the client as nervous as hell. But that's the ground you have got to break. More people see TV commercials than they do movies – and that's pretty wild.

Michael Bay

Elevator Fantasy   **Roman Era**

Levi's 'Elevator Fantasy'
1997

Diet Coke 'Roman Era'
1993

Director
Michael Bay

Producer
John Marias

Production Company
Propaganda Films

Production Manager
Nancy Sandberg

Director of Photography
Alan Daviau

Art Director
Mayne Berke

Director
Michael Bay

Producers
Phil Rose
Simon Straker

Production Company
Propaganda Films

Production Managers
D.J. Ford
Andrea Begley

Director of Photography
John Schwartzman

Art Director
Tom Faden

Bugle Boy 'Intro'
1992

Director
Michael Bay

Producer
Howard Woffinden

Production Company
Propaganda Films

Production Manager
Beth Galanty

Art Director
Deborah Evans

Michael Bay

Aaron Burr

Got Milk? 'Aaron Burr'
1994

Director
Michael Bay

Producer
Scott Gardenhour

Production Company
Propaganda Films

Production Manager
Andrea Begley

Director of Photography
Mark Plummer

Art Director
Don Burt

Nike 'Dr Rudolf'
1990

Director
Michael Bay

Producer
Simon Straker

Production Company
Propaganda Films

Production Manager
Mary Hamilton

Director of Photography
Jon Schwartzman

Art Director
Brian Jones

 After graduating with a degree in economics from Penn State University and studying at Cooper Union School of Design in New York, Bob Brooks worked as an art director in New York. He came to London as co-creative director at Benton & Bowles before starting his own photographic studio. With Len Fulford and Jim Baker, he went on to form the production company later known as BFCS, through which he directed many of his classic commercials. A co-founder of D&AD, he was awarded its President's Award in 1984. His work has earned him top prizes at Cannes, the London TV Awards, D&AD, the New York Clios, One Show and Art Directors Club. Voted Best Commercial Director in 1983 by the Directors Guild of America, Bob has also directed feature films ('The Knowledge' for Thames Television, 'Tattoo' for 20th Century Fox) and episodic television ('Space 1999').

When I began as an agency art director in New York I believed that design was the answer to successful advertising. I soon realised that the look of the ad was secondary to its real purpose... the message. This belief in content has shaped my career as a director of advertising films. I am primarily a story-teller.

It all began with a commercial for Senior Service Extra cigarettes from CDP, London. Before then I had been pigeon-holed as a food/table-top director. This spot was unlike anything I had directed up to that time. It was a charming script that relied entirely on acting. To my delight it produced a Gold Lion on my first try at Cannes, establishing my reputation as a director of humorous commercials. The spot was a rare blend of English and American humour and for the first time I experienced the skills of highly professional actors. A revelation!

I am an actor's director, yet I had no formal acting training or experience. Initially I was quite nervous dealing with actors, but the professionalism of most British actors soon helped me gain confidence. They have a marvellous attitude to their work. Their craft is acting and they are not afraid to try any medium, unlike most European actors who feel that advertising is to be avoided at all costs.

Casting sessions are of paramount importance. This is when you and the agency really discover the script. Dialogue that looks great on paper often falls flat when spoken. Sentimentality that might seem uncomfortable at first can often prove to be quite moving when spoken. I therefore spend a great deal of time with actors during casting sessions. Above all I rely heavily on my casting director. In my career I have used only a few. Half the battle is getting the right actors to the session. Only a casting director who is sensitive to you and your style can do it. I hate 'cattle calls', preferring a small number of well-chosen actors. I normally conduct the casting sessions, even to setting the lighting when possible. Except for the odd fashion or cosmetic assignment I very rarely use models.

Telling a complicated story in 30 to 60 seconds has made me a precise director. I am definitely not a 'shooter'. I seldom shoot wild shots hoping that somehow it will all come together in editing. I know what needs to be shot to produce the spot to length, though I always provide the editor with optional material, especially when the timings are very tight. There is nothing as satisfying as a cutaway that saves you three seconds. An accurate shooting

board with timings is developed after I have finished casting and have visited the set or location to clarify where and what I am going to shoot.

Because narrative commercials tend to be complicated I try to be very clear in execution and this brings me to the subject of continuity. I depend totally on accurate continuity. If someone is looking at another person off-camera from right to left, then the other person should respond looking left to right. Very basic... but if it's even slightly wrong, it may produce a second of doubt or confusion in the viewer's mind. In that time they may miss the next shot. That's what story-telling in 30 seconds is all about. Good script supervisors are priceless. When shots are only 1.5 seconds with dialogue or a specific action then accuracy is crucial. There is nothing worse than sitting in an edit suite and discovering that the script supervisor's timings are just a little off and no matter how hard you try, 32 seconds will not fit into a 30-second slot. Definitely not funny.

I always set my own shots, determining the lens size, angle and movement, all with editing in mind. At first I did my own lighting but I found that it weakened the actor/director relationship.

Performance is paramount and it may come in some unexpected way. The flick of an eyebrow; a body movement; the way a line is delivered. So placing the camera and keeping it there is vital. When I was an agency art director I worked with Irving Penn and learned an interesting technique. When Penn is faced with something elusive that he cannot predict, he will finalise everything that he can control, even to the point of nailing the camera to the floor, and then concentrate all his energy in capturing that elusive moment.

When I set a shot, I give actors as much information as possible. Then I let them get on with it and I look for the unexpected. When I did the Schweppes 'Subliminal Advertising' film with John Cleese, there was a moment when the stuffed animal heads on the wall behind Cleese had to say "Schweppes, Schweppes, Schweppes" and as he turns around, they were to stop abruptly. On the last take, there was one slight movement from the black panther head after Cleese turned. It was a mistake, but John just went up and stared at the head nose-to-nose trying to understand what he just saw. Finally he shrugged and turned back to the camera and continued his dialogue. The reaction had not been planned and for me it was the funniest moment in the commercial... pure Cleese.

I find the best performances come around take six or seven as actors usually need several takes to get the rhythm of the shot. The stopwatch is a terrible taskmaster. If the client or agency is not satisfied with the shot and their requests are valid, we continue, because sometimes you realise that you have misunderstood their intent for a particular shot or piece of copy.

What I hate most, however, is when the agency come up after the camera has been moved to a new setup and tell me that I should have done the last shot differently. With all the sophisticated playback equipment that now exists it is part of the agency's responsibility to follow the shooting carefully and know what is happening.

When I began working in advertising I realised I had found my true vocation. Everything I enjoy in life comes together in the medium: art, architecture, industrial design, fashion, typography, photography, film, literature, humour, food, travel and music. In fact, anything that you like or know about can be used. That's why you find people with all sorts of backgrounds doing really well in advertising. It's a great way to spend one's life!

Bob Brooks

Smash 'Martians'
1974

Agency
BMP, London

Senior Service Extra 'Tailor'
1968/69

Agency
Collett Dickenson Pearce, London

Heineken 'Nero'
1973

Agency
Collett Dickenson Pearce, London

Dr Pepper 'Godzilla'
1983

Agency
Young & Rubicam, New York

Martians, Tailor, Nero, Godzilla

Barclaycard 'Punk'
1979

Agency
Collett Dickenson Pearce, London

Hallmark Greeting Cards 'Music Professor'
1987/88

Agency
Young & Rubicam, New York

Hamlet Cigars 'Sidecar'
1980/81

Agency
Collett Dickenson Pearce, London

BT 'Mobile Phone'
1990/91

Agency
J. Walter Thompson, London

Bob Brooks

Oreo Cookies 'Facts of Life'
1988/89

Agency
Lieber Katz, New York

Schweppes 'Subliminal Advertising'
1990/91

Agency
Ammirati Puris Lintas

Pepsi Cola 'Diner'
1967/68

Agency
BMP, London

Hamlet 'Fancy Dress'
1987/88

Agency
Collett Dickenson Pearce, London

Olympus Cameras 'Grand Prix'
1984

Agency
Collett Dickenson Pearce, London

Benson & Hedges Small Cigars 'Istanbul'
1975

Agency
Collett Dickenson Pearce, London

Yellow Pages 'J.R. Hartley'
1984/85

Agency
Abbott Mead Vickers.BBDO, London

Bud

I see my work as a team effort where there's no distinction between writer, art director or director. Anybody can contribute to any part of the process. Most of my best work has been a collaboration between me and the agency at script stage. And it's great when that carries on through the shoot into post production.

A lot of trust has to be given to a director the team may hardly know and I guess having an agency background can be reassuring. The fact is I've got more agency experience than I ever meant to have which I suppose makes teams feel like they're talking to someone who understands what they've been through. But I think my experience behind the lens, operating and lighting, helps me understand the crew's side of things as well. The more a director can do himself (even if he chooses not to) the better his control of the overall picture. Just getting a good crew around you isn't enough. Besides, if you rely on particular technicians who then aren't available, you're lost.

I think the idea of the 'director's vision' is over-hyped. Often when I take a job on I'm not exactly sure how the finished ad is going to look. There's a million choices and decisions that have to be made along the way which will shape the final thing. No one really knows: all the director should do is know more than anyone else.

How I tend to work now is almost the opposite to the way I learned to make commercials at BMP. The discipline of making a tight animatic, the right time length, with recorded performances and dubbed soundtrack is invaluable. But by shooting around the idea you find that there's always other things that come up that you couldn't have anticipated. Three months before a shoot it's impossible to know what might come up in the casting, rehearsals, locations or editing. Things change constantly and if

you're with a good team who are open to that, when the idea is simple enough to allow some sort of flexibility, that's where the art comes in. That's what the director can really bring, a lot of stuff that's impossible to define.

That's not to say you can go in with some hidden agenda. The director has to be up-front and tell people what he wants to do. You can't ignore it's an ad. In fact you shouldn't want to. I think people feel cheated if they watch a commercial and don't get what the client wants to say about the product. And you shouldn't be able to take that product away from the idea. It won't work. As a piece of communication it will fall to bits.

To be honest I don't know if I actually enjoy making commercials. It's a sort of love-hate relationship. The actual process is more demanding than rewarding. I think the reward comes weeks later when people tell you they like it and you feel okay to look at it again.

I accept that it's difficult to pin me down.

People tell me that I've got no style at all, which I think is meant as a compliment. But I guess I've never really known what I wanted to do when I grew up. And I still feel that way. After art college I turned down an offer as a photographer to become an art director and got a job as copywriter. I never really wanted to be in advertising but after I took the job I wanted to show off as a writer so I'd write wall-to-wall dialogue commercials. When I started directing I wanted to show off photographically and did a lot of experimental visual stuff. I think that was something I needed to get off my chest. I'm all right again now.

Looking back I find it uncanny how, each time I've wanted to explore a particular area or style of film-making, that opportunity has arrived. I'm actually more surprised that I'm ever given work at all, based on that all-important first meeting. I'm usually terrible at them. I could never do a flashy presentation. Often I won't even know how I'm going to approach the job. There are usually so many options,

and I tend to overload on ideas that I'll eventually drop but haven't yet thought through properly. It's great if it's just a group of people talking through some ideas, but when it's a silent jury just sitting taking notes I want to walk out.

Most scripts aren't great. And all scripts can either get better or worse in the making. When you do take on a job it's amazing how much stuff is flying all around you that relates to that project. Until you're hired you're not even aware of it. My house is a maze of piles of videos, magazines, photographs and tear sheets and when you've got a job in mind it's amazing how things suddenly stick.

There has always been this debate about style and content, but there's no definitive answer. It's about balance. Technique can be superfluous, but cold reason can be soulless. Both need each other. In the end you have to let a piece of work kick you in the gut. I think too many people look for rules in advertising. It's not about that. You have to feel it, and often too much of it gets strangled by logic.

Some people say that advertising has changed for the worse over the years. I actually think it's got better. Okay there was a period in the late seventies when CDP and BMP were doing brilliant work and suddenly there was this cliff-face on the graph of creativity. It was advertising's equivalent to the Stones and the Beatles, and I don't think you can repeat that initial surge. But having said that, I don't think that was the peak, I think that things have got better since then.

At the moment there is a lack of well-written dialogue commercials but there's more humour, irreverence, and audacious visual style than there's ever been.

Advertising is so much more an accepted part of our society now. Magazines review the latest ads alongside films and records, and that's the way it should be. Something to be enjoyed and proud of. Something that crosses over into the real world. A respected part of our culture and not something to be looked down on.

Frank Budgen

Number One   Gun

Audi 'Number One'
1995
This actor got the job the moment he walked into the casting suite in his camel coat with the collar turned up. He was so right for the part I still don't know to this day whether he knew it was a send up or not.

Holsten Pils 'Gun'
1995
Denis Leary pulls out a 9mm Glock, loads it and sticks it straight into the lens. Blam! The ASA didn't like that. The original script referred to the brewers 'splashing Old Spice on a wrestler's balls'. The ASA weren't too keen on that either. Neither were Old Spice. Finally Denis shoots a guy, dead. Then calls him an asshole. By now even the client was getting cold feet. The ad never ran. It's Denis' favourite.

Pepe 'Tumble'
1995
The most laid-back client in the history of advertising. He didn't care if the cast wore Pepe clothes or not. Didn't bat an eye when the cut looked nothing like the script. And when I asked him what he thought of the finished ad (when I bumped into him at a Fugees concert) he replied, "Wicked".

Vauxhall 'A Different World'
1994
I filmed this commercial in Iceland which has a population of about 37. Though it looks hot, the half-dressed African women nearly froze to death. It was all shot in-camera, no post production tricks. We were going to do a scene that was supposed to be set in India but the only Indian guy on the island had emigrated a month ago.

Frank Budgen

Static

UFO

Capital Radio 'Static'
1996

I remember sitting in the pre-production meeting trying to explain to a couple of clients with terrified eyes and frozen smiles how this ad would finally look. They politely asked (their jobs on the line) if we thought the camera, which we were still trying to build at the time, would actually work. In my usual reassuring tone I told them "I don't know." And I wasn't lying.

Two days later we were dodging police round the streets of London with a 20ft lump of metal held together with Meccano and gaffer tape. With no viewfinder and no aperture control over the 125 instamatic lenses it was a case of using one elastic band to pull the shutter on a dull shot and two elastic bands on a bright one.

Incredibly, every shot was correctly exposed, and we used every frame.

VW Golf 'UFO'
1996

The original script for this revealed the car at the end and the first thing the client said to me was "Can we please get a good look at the car in this ad". I explained how in this instance I thought it would work much better if we never actually saw the car. We agreed to cover it, but when the client saw the cut with the Texan couple trying to describe this thing with a "vee dublya" on it, he never asked to see a cut with the car in it.

Centraal Beheer 'Museum'
1996
I'd made quite a few commercials this year that had either run into trouble with the ASA, been banned or restricted to cinema or MTV, so when I read the script for Centraal I thought, here we go again.

But the agency weren't about to let a little thing like the President of the United States of America spoil a good ad. So they never mentioned it to him.

John Clarke started his career in photography. His earliest success was a campaign for Lifelon stockings for the legendary Robert Brownjohn, which received one of the first D&AD awards. Before starting John S. Clarke Productions in 1982 he directed out of several production companies, including the late Terence Donovan's. Notable early campaigns included spots for VW and COI and Ronstrip 'Town Hall' which won a D&AD Silver. Irn Bru 'Culprit' in 1983 earned Golds at the BTAA and Creative Circle Awards and another D&AD Silver. His reputation was confirmed in 1987 with Audi 'Odd Couple' through BBH. Since 1991 Clarke has been synonymous with the popular series of Sainsbury's campaigns featuring the favourite recipes of TV celebrities. He is actively developing feature film scripts through his own company, Hero Films.

It's not so much what you look for in a script as what you hope for. Does it form opinions, is it breaking new ground, will it turn heads? Good ideas are sometimes quite hidden and you may not find the true value of the concept until you've lived with it for a while. It is important to value those early instinctive thoughts that inspire the imagination. They are almost subconscious and can be easily dismissed, but the most resonant of those thoughts are really worth hanging onto because they're often the key.

The conversion process from story to film is always fragile so it is worth remembering that part of the author is in the script. The creatives will have lived with the problem for a long time and they may well be tapping into something very personal – a childhood memory or perhaps something less easily explained. It is important for the film-maker to try to recognise and measure this. From those seeds you could uncover some valuable threads of poetry.

It's not a science: you're searching for a special blend of unknown elements. That creative aspect must be the director's foremost responsibility. If you take on the film you automatically take on a whole lot of other responsibilities. The pre-production meeting for example. As you're the interpreter you are best placed to explain and translate how the conversion of the idea will transfer to film. This responsibility can easily put you in the firing line and you can find yourself in the situation of discussing agency business outside of your terms of reference. It's a cleft stick. You're there to communicate your ideas and get a seal of approval. So you had better make sure you are close to the product because otherwise you can't defend, attack or debate when you're questioned on your views.

You're only ever as good as your behaviour – your performance. A director has to be master of many things but he relies an awful lot on the people around him and it is vital to have everyone's support. But the bottom line is that no one else is going to

drive these people when it's wet and the light is going and they're hungry. No one else is going to keep a hundred people out there at sub-zero temperatures. Only the director will do that. It's a slightly abnormal human condition. There aren't many commercial situations like that. It can appear indulgent but then that is also the nature of what we're doing and the excesses sometimes break new frontiers.

I'm a very hands-on director. For me it's essential to be involved with the camera. Looking through the camera is the only true way to gauge performances, and I'm constantly involved with the imagery – that's the only way I can operate. I'm extremely focused but I'm always open to ideas. If you're too autocratic people aren't inclined to help when it matters. You can never have enough eyes on the set. It's important to have the right atmosphere so that any member of the team can make an observation. The tap on the shoulder when you're deep in concentration can be the hardest thing to deal with – but that

tap could be the key to something more interesting.

I think that new technology is there to take advantage of and make life more interesting – but not to pay homage to. It's probably a bad period to be in to some extent because of the enormous, ever-increasing, variety of media that advertisers can invest in. Everybody's always harking back saying how wonderful everything was 25 years ago: there were very simple ideas, executed in a very simple way. But they were appropriate for that particular time. Now you have different responsibilities and consequently writing is more emotive and textured.

Readjustment is a common need in a contemporary world. As a photographer going into film-making I knew nothing about narrative and needed to become a student of it. Since becoming involved in feature film scripts I've developed another area of sensitivity that didn't exist before. The conditions that allow the 30-second commercial to prosper are changing, it's a fact of life. You can't complain about

it. One has to change the rules to allow certain things to flourish in a different way.

My reasons for being in commercials are quite selfish. The format allows me to enjoy all the things I like doing: film-making, photography, inventing, the cinema, the theatre. I have quite eclectic tastes and views and advertising always allows me to discover something new. It's tremendous.

By nature I'm always searching. I think we all are. It's an itch. I just think that some people forget how to do it. But I think searching keeps you fresh and you're always uncovering something new.

Before viewing the following pages it is worth considering the sound that goes with the pictures and the importance of music. The choice and execution of the music is a valuable ingredient and should never be underestimated. At its best it enhances all of the essential flavours in the film, and can elevate it to another dimension. It has much to do with the film's success and it's very rewarding when you get it right.

John S. Clarke

Odd Couple

Culprit

Audi 'Odd Couple'
1987
A demonstration to illustrate that people are closely observed to aid car design.

Music
Mozart Sonata No 12

Irn Bru 'Culprit'
1983
One way of finding who's been drinking Irn Bru is to use a magnet.

Refresher Course

The Visit

10 kinds of egg.

Sainsbury's 'Refresher Course'
1997
A celebration of the freshness of food.

Music
Louis Armstrong: 'I'm Putting All My Eggs in One Basket'

Barclays Bank 'The Visit'
1997
A comparison between banking today and how it used to be. The home banker reflects back to when he was a child and went to the bank with his father.

Music
The Kinks: 'Tired of Waiting'

37 kinds of fish on our fresh fish counters.

8 kinds of pear.

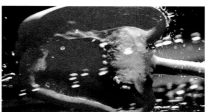

10 kinds of olive.

4 kinds of pepper.

17 kinds of organic fruit & veg.

6 kinds of chilli.

1 kind of star fruit.

John S. Clarke

Pretty Polly 'The Shot'
1988
The inventor of Nylon is commemorated by featuring a female photographer taking his portrait in the 1940s. She removes her stocking and puts it over the lens to improve the image.

Music
Ray Noble: 'The Very Thought of You'

British Rail 'Hush Hour'
1988
The commuters are dancers; their tap echoes the phrase 'Gotta go to work, gotta go to work.' The after rush-hour commuters tap to 'Cheaper ticket, cheaper ticket'.

Music
Tap: hushed chanting of the above themes

GM Card 'Sign Here'
1993
American testimonials about a credit card that is to be launched in the UK.

Music
Aaron Copeland: 'Fanfare to the Common Man'

Standard Life 'Colourful Life'
1993
A series of cameos that, with the aid of a caption, justify a particular 'life'.

Music
Black: 'Wonderful Life'

Gla

After completing a degree in theatre design and direction, Jonathan Glazer worked in a company making trailers for films and videos. In 1991, this led on to a job directing and writing television promos and idents. Sponsored by his present production company, Academy, he made two shorts in 1993 which helped to launch him as a director of commercials and music videos. His work includes spots for Nike, AT&T, Levi's, Carling Premier, Club Med, Reebok and VW and promos for Massive Attack, Blur, Nick Cave and his multi-award-winning videos for Radiohead and Jamiroquai. In 1995, he won Best Director at the Midsummer Advertising Awards.

You are defined as much by the work you turn down as the work you take on. When I started directing commercials, I decided only to do work which was related to where my head is. I'm fascinated by people, and film is 100% about people and our humanity. If a script doesn't say anything to me on a personal, emotional level, then it ain't worth doing. It's just cosmetic. There's a place for that, but not in my heart – and that's where I work from.

I treat commercials as if they are films. I get frustrated when I go into a meeting and the creatives ask me how it's going to look, whether I'm going to do anything funky with it. I'll say, "can we just talk about the story and the character first?" And I think they are often quite surprised that I take the story so seriously, but everything comes out of that.

I'm a great believer in what isn't said – what is understated or enigmatic. The scripts I shot for AT&T were clever pieces of underwritten dialogue. They gave me a very free canvas to get to the heart of the people they were about. For instance, the woman whose husband doesn't spend enough time with her, whose lifestyle appears enviable but is sterile and manicured – empty. I could reflect that idea in every aspect of the film-making, from the casting to the choice of location. I think those films were well received because they were truthful. The people were imperfect. I'm much more interested in tapping into imperfection as a film-maker than in making things so perfect that they alienate you.

Because everything in my work revolves around the people in the frame, casting is obviously my first port of call in terms of what I'm trying to get right. The script of AT&T 'Employee' featured a woman saying "No" in reply to three questions; so it was all about the subtext. I wanted a very specific kind of face with a slightly rejected look. I looked at hundreds of girls in England, Romania and France before I found Judy Kleinman, who had an intriguing face and eyes that were just so full of life and experience and pathos. Some people have a cinematic quality. They're not necessarily beautiful, but when they're on screen you can't take your eyes off them. That's what I'm after. Sometimes, before we

shoot, people look at my choices and say, "are you sure about her? She'd be alright for a film, but her face won't read in a commercial". I think that's untrue. An unusual look can be so much more powerful than the ridiculous square-jawed stereotypes you see in so many commercials. Judy in 'Employee' was hailed in the national press because she appeared at a time when women over the age of 35 thought they were being rejected, not considered sexy or worthy of being protagonists in advertising.

I storyboard, but really more for my own thought process than any other reason. If I don't draw then I won't have been through that first process of rationalising why you're shooting something. As my producer says of me, I never like to be more than 75% prepared. I need that other 25% to be unprepared so that I can use my instincts. The storyboard lays down the building blocks of the story so that then I'll know where I can deviate from it, embellish or change it when I'm shooting.

Shooting can be a pain in the arse. It entails a whole series of creative compromises as a result of

circumstances beyond your control – that dress you wanted didn't turn up, or this actor cut his hair the day before the shoot, or it's raining when we didn't want it to. But on the other hand, there's a sharpness that comes from working with less control. You have to respond to all the accidents. So if it is raining and that's wrong, you stage the scene in a doorway and that gives it a whole different resonance. Making a film is an organic thing and you have to be big enough to move with it if you want to make something worthwhile and truthful. If you just stand there and say, "no, this is where the camera's got to be, that's where the girl's got to be, we'll wait till the bloody rain stops...", you're going to land up with soap powder commercials on your showreel.

I don't believe in being unusual for the sake of being unusual. If you use an effect, there should be a reason for it. Images should be used to give voice to thoughts. When I did the 'Street Spirit' promo for Radiohead, I wanted to evoke a very specific feeling – how when you dream, you never seem to arrive, something else always begins to happen just as you

reach your destination. So I needed an effect that would make you feel like that. I wasn't the first person to use a photosonic camera, but it became associated with me because I tried to use it expressively and in a dramatic context. When I used it again in the Nike 'Jordan – Frozen Moment' film, it seemed the perfect way to express the idea that when Michael Jordan plays, the whole world slows to standstill to watch him.

In advertising, there's some amazing stuff around, but the majority is lowest common denominator. A lot of people see my stuff and probably say, "good film-maker, but doesn't know the first thing about commercials". I don't think that would be unfair. Commercials don't turn me on because they're commercials, but because they're films. And I've been very lucky. I arrived in advertising at a time when the business was beginning to favour more eclectic directors. The industry has been like a benefactor. I've had some fantastic opportunities to make films that have allowed me to develop my own sensbility.

Jonathan Glazer

Protection

Kung Fu

VW Polo 'Protection'
1997

Levi's 'Kung Fu'
1997

Art Director
Jeremy Craigen

Art Director
Tony McTear

Copywriter
Jeremy Craigen

Copywriter
Jeremy Carr

Agency
BMP DDB Needham

Agency
Bartle Bogle Hegarty

Lighting Cameraman
Steve Keith Roach

Lighting Cameraman
Steve Keith Roach

Editor
John McManus @ OBE

Editor
Rick Lawley @ The White House

Producer
Nick Morris

Producer
Nick Morris

Production Company
Academy

Production Company
Academy

Street Spirit   **Virtual Insanity**

Radiohead 'Street Spirit'   Jamiroquai 'Virtual Insanity'
1995   1996

Commissioner
Dilly Gent

Commissioner
Mike O'Keefe

Record Company
Parlophone

Record Company
Sony

Lighting Cameraman
Steve Keith Roach

Lighting Cameraman
Steve Keith Roach

Editor
John McManus @ OBE

Producer
Nick Morris

Producer
Nick Morris

Production Company
Academy

Production Company
Academy

Jonathan Glazer

Employee

New York

AT&T 'Employee'
1996

Caffreys 'New York'
1995

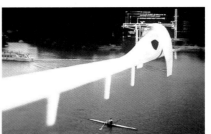

Art Director
Roger Ackerman

Copywriter
Jerry Green

Agency
McCann-Erickson

Lighting Cameraman
Ivan Bird

Editor
John McManus @ OBE

Producer
Nick Morris

Production Company
Academy

Creative Directors
Larry Barker
Rooney Carruthers

Agency
WCRS

Lighting Cameraman
Ivan Bird

Editor
Rick Lawley @ The White House

Producer
Nick Morris

Production Company
Academy

Gridlock Frozen Moment

Carling Premier 'Gridlock'
1995

Nike 'Frozen Moment'
1996

Creative Directors
Larry Barker
Rooney Carruthers

Agency
WCRS

Lighting Cameraman
Ivan Bird

Editor
Rick Lawley @ The White House

Producer
Nick Morris

Production Company
Academy

Art Director
Larry Fry

Copywriter
Jamie Barrett

Agency
Wieden & Kennedy

Editor
Emily Dennis
@ Mad River, LA

Lighting Cameraman
Max Malkin

Producer
Nick Morris

Production Company
Propaganda, LA

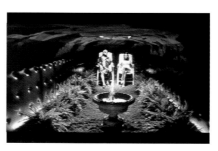 

Gor

Michel Gondry studied graphic arts in Paris before forming a rock band with friends. He shot the group's videos using animation and live action filmed on his own 16mm camera. This led to other promo work for French artists. His reputation established, Gondry went on to make videos for international artists such as Björk, Massive Attack, Daft Punk, Foo Fighters and the Rolling Stones, among others. He was awarded Best Director at the MTV Awards 1996 and a D&AD Silver for most outstanding pop video for the Rolling Stones. He won Gold and Silver awards for Levi's 'Drugstore,' 'Mermaids' and Polaroid 'Resignation'.

I went into music videos in the most natural way. I was playing in a band called Oui Oui and my child-hood heroes were Meliès, Norman McLaren, Charlie Chaplin and East European animators. So I bought a camera and had my first experience of animation trying to illustrate our music. Then, little by little, I integrated human beings into my universe. I always preferred to find my own way to achieve my ideas instead of asking anybody, so I developed personal techniques and always was able to find ideas that I could execute myself.

From the beginning, my goal was to complete the universe of the music with my images, not to stick them over the song. Discussion with the rest of the band was very important as they wanted to be involved in the visuals. I learned how to confront and combine ideas in the interest of the films. My musi-cian's background has helped me immensely with my relationship with artists.

I did six videos for my own band, before I started working for other artists. For a while, it was difficult to find people on the same wavelength to work with until I met Björk. Then it was possible again to do the most personal ideas but this time with more money.

In the video 'Hyperballad', Björk wanted to be dead and alive at the same time. I came up with the idea that she has just thrown herself from a cliff-top and we see a close up of her dead face – then her soul appears superimposed with a low video resolu-tion, like an antique hologram. This mixture of high-tech and low-tech is something Björk and I always liked. The promo is like a super low-tech video game, like the first one that ever existed where a half mirror was used to mix a simple video animation to a miniature landscape.

By contrast, in the Rolling Stones video I used a modern technique (morphing and CGI) to give a

different dimension to a hallucinogenic effect that has been done many times before in a more classical way.

It was easy for me to take the step from doing promos to advertising, as I had learned with my band to share ideas. When the story is not mine, I try to find the essence of it to make it stronger and always use my visuals to enhance the story, never to give a special look.

For example in the Polaroid commercial, the creatives wanted to use time-lapse footage to show the feeling of being oppressed by the city. I didn't want to use this existing technique, so I tried to take it a step further. After finishing the Rolling Stones video where I used morph to transform point of view, I proposed we combine the old time-lapse technique with my morph technique. It worked and we managed to create the feeling of somebody who's so sick of the office and the city, he's banging his head against the walls.

I approach my work with quite a strong philosophy. I hated advertising in the 80s. It was all about the cult of personality, everybody was beautiful and it made you feel bad not to be trendy or slick. I think there is beauty in ordinary people, in real life, and if you show that in advertising the viewers feel they are part of the world. They are not despised by the makers of the product, no one is forcing them to be something they aren't.

A perfect example is the Levi's 'Drugstore' commercial. The Levi's hero was always so beautiful and muscle-bound that I hated it. Anyway it would have been difficult to do a commercial with this type of hero because my old band mates would refuse to talk to me anymore! So here I had a good excuse. It was the American depression and the film had to look authentic, otherwise, it would be silly. So the guy couldn't be like a super hunk. The overall old aspect of the film is done in-camera. Actually every-

body was freaking out when they were watching me shaking the camera speed control like mad but it was the only way to achieve it.

In my recent commercial for Smirnoff I tried to do an epic adventure in one minute. One of my contributions was how to change the perspective to create more surprising transitions through the bottle. An example is the vertical wall of the hotel becoming the horizontal deck of the boat. I wanted to give the film a light spirit even though you feel danger is always around the corner. I don't think strength and originality depends on dark and depressing images.

My mum came to the shooting of the Levi's 'Mermaids' commercial and I overheard her in the middle of a really embarrassing conversation with the agency producer – "he's my son, I always knew that he was special." The producer replied, "after Michel worked for us on 'Drugstore' everyone knew that". I couldn't interrupt because I was hiding in the bushes.

Michel Gondry

Björk 'Hyperballad'
1996
We superimposed in-camera 14 times on the same piece of film, without being able to control anything. Exhausting! It is the last of the four videos I made for Björk.

Levi's 'Drugstore'
1995
To give a 1920s 'depression years' aspect, we got rid of the usual glamour look of Levi's. My father never forgave me for the blurred shot of the little girl.

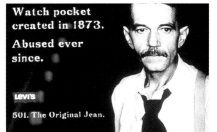

Mermaids　　　Resignation

Levi's 'Mermaids'
1997
When my friends saw the film they said to me, "We didn't know that you could do something sexy!"
"That's easy," I replied.

Polaroid 'Resignation'
1996
The young man is so sick of his office and his city that he feels as if he's banging his head against the walls. To give this impression, I made this non-stop, side-to-side movement, which was added in post production.

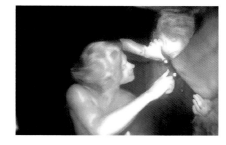

Michel Gondry

Smirnoff 'Smarienberg'
1997
When I presented the storyboard, everybody thought
that it would be impossible to shoot. They were
nearly right but I wanted to try it.

The Rolling Stones 'Like a Rolling Stone'
1996
This was the first time that my father complimented
me. "Giant!" he said – I still haven't recovered.

56

I said...   **Around the World**

Volvo 'I said...'
1996
The creatives were thinking of something in the Tarantino style ... I thought that 'Die Hard' was more fun.

Daft Punk 'Around the World'
1997
Each group of characters represents an instrument from the song. They create the choreography by looping in the track.

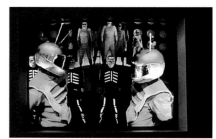

Go

After studying at the Ecole Nationale Supérieure des Arts Décoratifs and working as an illustrator in Paris, Jean-Paul Goude went to New York to become *Esquire* magazine's art editor. From 1978 to 1982, he was Grace Jones' artistic director and manager, conceiving and directing her shows and promo videos. Subsequently, he returned to France and began to direct commercials. His award-winning work for Lee Cooper, Orangina, Kodak, Citroën, Perrier and Chanel established him as one of the leading directors and stylists in Europe. In 1989, he designed and directed 'La Marseillaise', the opera-ballet centrepiece of the French Bicentennial celebrations and was awarded the Légion d'Honneur by President Mittérand. He has also redesigned France's Channel 5, staged fashion shows for Azzedine Alaia and published several books featuring his graphics, illustrations, costume and set designs.

My Mother always said, "an artist's work is a reflection of his soul." I took that literally, and when as a teenager I began to think about what I wanted to do, I took an inventory of what was going on around me to find a medium through which I might be able to express myself. Abstract painting was all the rage when I was a student, but what really inspired me were the magazines we received at home from the States – *Esquire*, *Bazaar*, *Life*. I fell in love with the pictures, the graphics, even the ads – and I decided this was going to be the premise for my artistic life.

The root of my work is based on a personal mythology drawn from childhood experiences. Mom is Irish-American, a ballet dancer who came to live in France when she met my father. She was always regaling me with stories about Broadway shows and Harlem jazz. New York became my promised land. Closer to home, the area in which we lived in Paris had been rebuilt to celebrate France's colonies on the eve of the 1930 World Fair; the exoticism and eroticism of foreign lands was still 'à la mode'. As I was growing up in the 50s, the Museum of the

Colonies was the centre of the neighbourhood. Its magnificent art déco façade featured sculptures of naked African, Asian and even Arab natives which I'm sure partly explains my preference for exotic women and my fascination with the human body. I also remember there was a zoo nearby; we would hear lions roaring in the hot summer nights. It was like a call to adventure. Last, I was an avid reader of comics as a kid – an influence which pervades my work.

Women are the real motivating force in my life, and I have always tried to seduce them through my work. First it was Mother. Her opinion was essential and I'd systematically take her my latest drawing for approval. Then came my girlfriends, and now my wife. I've never been much of an adventurer, yet through my passion for the mysterious morphologies of the women I loved, I did an awful lot of travelling and learned a great deal about foreign cultures.

Some have called me a Pygmalion... I'm not! Pygmalion fell in love with a statue to the extent that she came to life. I fell in love with real women

whom I tried to turn into statues. No wonder most of my relationships turned sour. My romance with Grace Jones is a perfect example of what I'm trying to say; was it Grace whom I fell in love with, or was it the idea of her? In any case, from 1978 to 1982, she represented the perfect vehicle for my work. Of course, it isn't healthy to express oneself through another human being, or conducive to a happy life. My conscious mind told me it was wrong, but my unconscious drive was more powerful. Yet, out of these fantasies came some of the best work.

My first commercial, for Lee Cooper, was a continuation of the shows I'd done for Grace – a mini-opera with a group of stylised, comic-book characters performing a dance which ended with a huge 'blue jeans' curtain being drawn by a giant zipper. I don't think that whatever success I may have had in advertising was due to my experience as a clever ad man, I simply think it happened because I let myself go and for better or for worse, created my own vocabulary.

You could say that I'm a bit of a show-off.

(Remember James Brown yelling "Look at me work!" as he would break into a dance routine? I'm a bit like that!) I do my best work when I have the impression that all eyes are on me. That's kind of what happened with Jacques Helleu from Chanel (the Diaghilev of the perfume world) when he called me in one day and dared me to come up with a film for 'Egoïste'.

My stock was riding high after the Bicentennial celebrations, and he gave me carte blanche to do whatever I wanted. The commercial was a happy marriage of style and content. The content came from the idea of women deploring male egotism. The style was provided by a device I'd come up with earlier for an aborted opera project set in France in an Arab neighbourhood. Here the Islamic women weren't allowed to go out, but saw everything going on in the street through the shutters. Every time they witnessed something they didn't like, they'd open the windows and protest in Arabic.

I'm at my best when I'm allowed a free rein – as with Helleu and with some of the other creative directors who allow me to conceive as well as execute my own work; which essentially means that I like to be in control of every aspect of the film, from the sets and the costumes, to the editing and even to the music production.

I'm at my worst when I'm up against 'creative' people, who not only know very little about visuals, but also try to tell me what I can and can't do by hiding behind the notion that they are the only ones who know what the customer wants. If Helleu had gone round the world 'overtesting' our commercials, they would have been killed.

At the end of the day, as Mom always said, you have to be yourself.

Beware of being too clever and too slick. It's your own idiosyncracies that make you and your work unique. The things which may seem unimportant to you, even a hindrance – they can be the most treasurable aspects of your personality, the ones which you should cultivate.

I know that may sound like a paradox, but it's certainly been the truth in my case.

Jean-Paul Goude

Family
Olympic Games

Kodak 'Family'
1984
An imagined French family on vacation is being photographed at the pool-side. The family's three daughters jump too far out and, missing the pool, they fall out of their Kodak transparency.

Agency
Young & Rubicam

Conceived and directed by
Jean-Paul Goude

Kodak 'Olympic Games'
1987
The three daughters are now famous; the French public has baptised them 'Kodakettes'. In this episode, the girls 'crash' the Olympics. After winning the 100 yards dash, they dive into the 'high-diving' pool, cheered by the Olympic public.

Agency
Young & Rubicam

Conceived and directed by
Jean-Paul Goude

Egoïste No 1
Egoïste No 2

Chanel 'Egoïste No 1'
1991
A luxurious hotel somewhere on the French Riviera.
Beautiful angry women, lyrically deplore masculine
egotism.

Conceived and directed by
Jean-Paul Goude

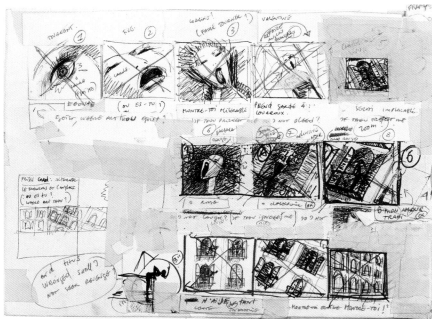

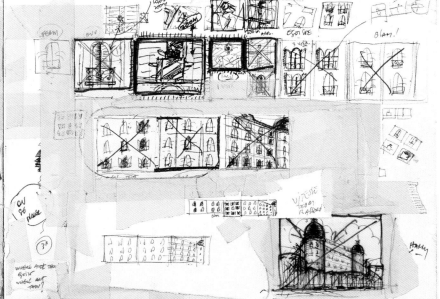

Chanel 'Egoïste No 2'
1991
Alone in the fancy suite of his French Riviera hotel,
drenched in 'Egoïste' eau de toilette, our vain egotist
is 'shadow-boxing'. Jealous, the 'shadow' complains:
"Why shouldn't it smell as good as its master?" In an
attempt to steal the bottle of perfume away, the
shadow hits its master who hits it back!

Conceived and directed by
Jean-Paul Goude

**Matador
The Lion**

Diam's 'Matador'
1988
In this tale, a female matador performs her 'death dance' in front of an enthusiastic audience of bulls.

Agency
Publicis

Conceived and directed by
Jean-Paul Goude

Perrier 'The Lion'
1994
Somewhere under the blazing African sun, a lost and thirsty explorer spots a Perrier bottle on a hill; so does a thirsty lion who in an attempt to intimidate the explorer, roars at her furiously. Unimpressed, the explorer roars back even louder, scaring the beast away.

Agency
Ogilvy & Mather

Conceived and directed by
Jean-Paul Goude

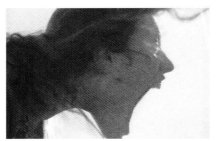

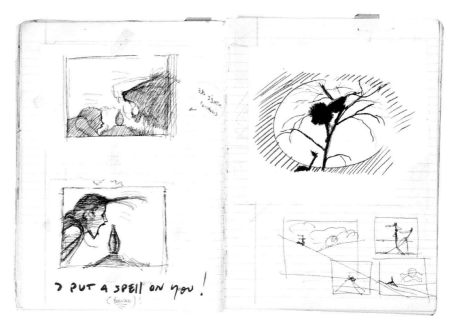

Coco
Eau d'Eden

Chanel 'Coco'
1993
Paris. Hotel Ritz – interior: night. The legend says that on some stormy summer nights, Mademoiselle Chanel's spirit comes back to haunt her empty, yet perfectly preserved apartments.

Conceived and directed by
Jean-Paul Goude

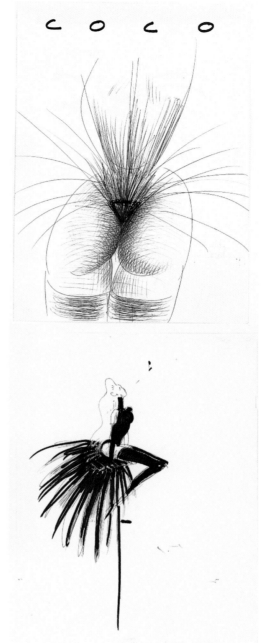

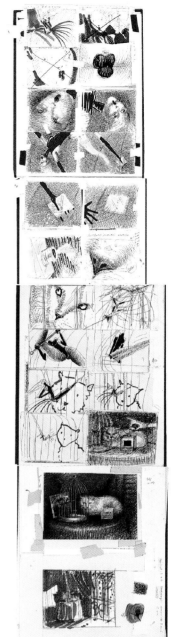

Cacharel 'Eau d'Eden'
1996
Somewhere in paradise, long before the 'apple' incident: the birth of Eve.

Conceived and directed by
Jean-Paul Goude

Jerry Hibbert first developed an interest in animation while studying at Ealing School of Art. After graduating, he worked at TV Cartoons where the commission to animate 'The South Bank Show' title sequence enabled him to set up his own production company. In 1983, with his reputation in advertising growing, he teamed up with Graham Ralph to form Hibbert Ralph Animation. He has won one D&AD Gold Award, seven Silvers, two Creative Circle Golds, four Silvers and a Clio Gold.

When I entered the business I worked under George Dunning, the director of 'Yellow Submarine'. He was always experimenting, so I was trained in an environment where I was constantly encouraged to do new things. That's the appeal of making commercials. I like moving between a variety of styles. You might be working on a very heavy 3D job, then go onto an untechnical, character-based film, then move onto something where you're blending animation with live action.

The first thing I do is make sure that I can tell the story properly in the allotted time, usually 30 seconds. It's nice to have a script which is slightly underwritten – that gives me the freedom to add the nuances of performance. With the Unison commercial, the script was pretty nailed down and there was an animatic. What wasn't nailed down was the bear's performance, how he reacts, what he does.

Sometimes I'll act a character out on the carpet by my desk if I need to work out where my weight would be in a funny walk or in some reaction. If there's music, that can give you a lot of inspiration before you put pen to paper. Or else the inspiration may come from reference material. For example, with the Adidas commercial, the idea was to draw a parallel between Del Piero the footballer and Del Piero the Renaissance artist. We couldn't find a Del Piero painting that suited what we wanted to do, so I used Duccio's 'Passion of Christ' instead. Each panel depicted scenes in which the perspectives were distorted so that what would have happened in a huge space was compressed into a twelve-foot area. I applied this effect to the idea of a football match.

I always rough the whole commercial out and

then shoot it with a guide track – usually my own voice. So you can get to a position very quickly where you've got something with sound and movement – the leica. You can make sure the story is clear. If something isn't working, it gives you an early warning. And it enables the client to make sure he's satisfied with the size of the product shot and the message he wants to get across. I respect what the client wants. I'm not much of a one for hiding packs in the background. At the end of the day, he's paying you to flog his stuff.

You cannot rely on happy accident in animation. A live-action director might go out and shoot hours of footage and then start chopping it around in the hope that something in there works. Animators plan everything out beforehand. That ability can come in handy for live action. When I did

the Adidas commercial, Del Piero was only available for one day in Milan. We couldn't take all the actors to Italy so we had to shoot on two separate days and blend everything together in post production. It all had to be thought out in advance – you couldn't have cobbled it up as you went along.

Two abilities make up the animator's craft. First is the ability to draw – fast, and in a lot of different styles. People who tend to be good at drawing tend to be good because they've looked at something and remembered it visually. I wonder how many people have seen the front of a Toyota Corolla car every day for the last ten years, but couldn't actually sit down and draw it because they hadn't observed it. The second ability is characterisation. We cast animators like you'd cast an actor. You can give one animator the scenario of a character walking down the street

and slipping on a banana skin and it will look rather painful and sad. And you can give it to another and he'll make it hilarious. So you expect a performance from your animator. If the first take isn't right, you get the animator to adjust it until it fulfills the idea you originally laid out in the leica.

Most work that comes into the studio can be inspiring. You try to give every job your best shot. Even in the old washing powder commercial, there is always some technical thing you did that was a success. No one else will see it, but you can sit down and say "actually what we did to make bubbles look good worked pretty well." You can get a lot of pleasure in some technical success. There's a saying in animation that you've got to be two out of three things – good, fast, reliable. If you're two, you'll always get by. If you're all three, you'll do bloody well.

Toshiba 'London – New York'
1996

Queen 'Innuendo'
1990

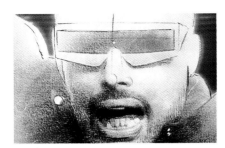

Director
Jerry Hibbert

Directors
Jerry Hibbert
Rudi Dolezal

Production Company
Hibbert Ralph Animation

Production Companies
Hibbert Ralph Animation
DoRo Productions

Producer
Maddy Sparrow

Producers
Carl Grinter
Hannes Rossacher

3D Operators/Animators
Natalie Zita
Elaine Foley
Chi Kwong-Lo
Jules Findley
Julian Serpell

Editors
Karen Bruce
Klaus Hundsbichler
Wolfgang Frank

Editors
Paul Coppock
Steve Hughes

Lighting Camerman
Peter Jefferies

2D Animators
Richard Fawdrey
Andrew Painter

Animators
Hilary Audus
Alan Bassett
Anna Brockett
Mike Church
Steve Weston
Celia Coppock
Gethyn Davies

2D Animation Assistants
Richard Wake
David Burns

Mac Operators
Gethyn Davies
Paul Tuersley

Animation Assistants
Iain McCall
Rob Hanson

**Reference
Background Artist**
Michael Bennallack-Hart

Clay Animation
Ted Berenson

Henry
Chris Mortimer
@ FrameStore

Video Post Production
Framestore

Agency
Duckworth Finn Grubb Waters

Video Editor
Colin Green

Art Director
Mike London

Harry Operator
Ian Bryers

Copywriter
James Fryer

Video Editor
Michael Hudecek

Producer
Kate O'Mulloy

Motion Control
Cell Animation

Creative Directors
Dave Waters/Paul Grubb

Rostrum Camera
Animated Opticals
Phil Campbell
Ray Clayton

Client
Toshiba

Dolls
Limitless Limited
Jeffrey Fineberg
Ted Berenson

Golden Valley Pop Pop 'Elephant'
1993

Adidas 'The Artist'
1996

Director
Jerry Hibbert

Production Company
Hibbert Ralph Animation

Producer
Fiona Plumstead

Character Design
Paul Driessen

Editors
Paul Coppock
Karen Bruce
Steve Hughes

Animators
Jerry Hibbert
Gethyn Davies
Richard Wake

Animation Assistants
Maoiliosa Kiely
Rob Hanson

Rostrum Camera
Animated Opticals
(Digital Rostrums)Ltd

Video Post Production
FrameStore

Operator
Tim Webber

Agency
WCRS

Producer
Vanessa Pickford

Copywriter
Andy Brittain

Art Director
Sandy Barker

Client
Golden Valley
Sharwoods (UK Distributors)

Director
Jerry Hibbert

Production Company
Hibbert Ralph Animation

Producer
Maddy Sparrow

Editors
Paul Coppock
Steve Hughes

Lighting Camera
Maxim Ford

Mac Operator
Karen Bruce

Costume Designer
Diana Moseley

Henry
Tim Osbourne
Tim Greenwood
@ FrameStore

Background paintings
David Millen

Agency
Leagas Delaney

Creative Director
Tim Delaney

Art Director
Dave Beverley

Copywriter
Rob Burleigh

Producer
Helen Williams

Client
Adidas

Product
Traxion

American Airlines 'Open Door'
1997

Post Office 'Fence'
1990

Director (Live Action & 3D)
Jerry Hibbert

Producer (Live Action & 3D)
Bernadette Napleton

Art Director
Gethyn Davies

Lighting Cameraman
Maxim Ford

3D Operators/Animators
Natalie Zita
Elaine Foley
Julian Serpell

Scenes 6 & 7
Paul Kavanagh
@ FrameStore

Mac Textures/Backgrounds
Karen Bruce
Paul Tuersley

Rendering
Dennis Sutton

Editors
Steve Hughes
Paul Coppock

Henry
Tim Osbourne
@ FrameStore

Agency
DDB Needham, Dallas

Director
Jerry Hibbert

Production Company
Hibbert Ralph Animation

Producer
Carl Grinter

Film Editor
Paul Coppock

Animators
Jerry Hibbert
Gethyn Davies

Animation Assistants
Rob Hanson
Iain McCall
Shelley McIntosh
Wendy Russell

Rendering Co-ordinator
Dennis Sutton

Rostrum Camera
Peter Jones Rostrums

Video Post Production
Ian Bryers
@ FrameStore

Agency
Gold Greenlees Trott

Producer
Penny Hiller

Art Director
Damon Collins

Copywriter
Mary Wear

Client
Post Office Counters

Unison 'Ant'
1995

Director
Jerry Hibbert

Production Company
Hibbert Ralph Animation

Producer
Bernadette Napleton

Editors
Paul Coppock
Steve Hughes

Animators
Gethyn Davies
Jerry Hibbert

Animation Assistant
Gary Kerr

Paint & Trace
Animo –
Penny Crowther
Oliver Cook

Video Post Production
FrameStore

Operator
Tim Greenwood

Agency
BMP DDB Needham

Producer
Anni Cullen

Copywriter
Nick Gill

Executive Creative Director
John Webster

Client
Unison

Since entering the film industry in 1962, Hugh Hudson has made feature films, documentaries and commercials, winning top prizes in all three areas. His films for Dubonnet, Levi's, Benson & Hedges, Fiat Strada, Courage and COI have all won D&AD and Television awards. Levi's 'Bottoms' won the Grand Prix in Venice and Coly L'Aimant, the Grand Prix in Cannes. 'Tortoise & Hare' (a forty-minute film for Pirelli) won First Prize in the Venice Documentary Festival. 'Chariots of Fire' was awarded four US Academy Awards; 'Greystoke' was nominated for five. His commercials were produced by Ridley Scott Associates between 1970 and 1975. Since then he has headed his own production company, Hudson Film, through which he also produces his feature films and made his seven Labour Party election films in 1987 and 1992.

I made my first film aged eight – a family affair 'Roundheads v Cavaliers'. From the age of ten, I realised I was going to be a feature film director, an anarchic one at that. But in the 50s, the industry was a closed shop. Completely nepotistic.

I tried every single film studio. Every major producer. The door was slammed every time. So television commercials, which were just starting, were a means to an end. You need to practise your trade on a daily basis. I'm an artisan. I was apprenticed in the cutting rooms. Learn a trade. You'll make a better table if you practise carpentry.

When I made commercials in the 70s, we were always drawing from feature films. Stealing ideas, copying styles. Alan Parker, Ridley Scott, myself. We were making 30-second films. Stories with characters and dialogue, little comedic anecdotes like the Cinzano commercials I did with Leonard Rossiter and Joan Collins, 60-second situation comedies with

Arthur Lowe, Michael Horden, June Whitfield. That form of advertising has gone completely now. MTV created a new demand for aggression and speed. Any image goes. It only has to be on screen long enough to catch the eye.

Directors now are another breed. What would you call them? Electro-computocrats. Not filmmakers. They rely on the post production house to make their film for them. But I believe human drama/comedic commercials will come back. They're about relationships and emotions and ultimately that's all that's important.

Enjoy fighting for a job. The thrill of the chase. Persuading the client. Knocking out the competition – it's poker. When I was put up to do the Marines, they refused to let an Englishman loose on this quintessentially American institution. I had to fly to Atlanta twice, do big presentations, bring the budget down to be competitive. I won them over. They

loved the commercial. It swept the board at the Möbius Awards, I was made an honorary member of the US Marines.

If I'd lived in the last century I would probably have been a commissioned painter. Painting a family's house or a portrait. My films show I have ability to handle epic scenes. My job is to embellish an idea and make it doubly interesting. When you've got characters, the most important thing is casting. After that, getting the right location is critical. Go on and on looking for locations until you run out of time. There's always something better.

Horse power. If you have a weak horse you won't reach the line. Strong actors. Strong technicians. For instance, when I did Courage 'Gertcha', I got Bob Krasker, who shot 'The Third Man', out of retirement to light it. He did a fantastic job. One shot. Sepia. Beautifully lit. So employ the best people. Involve them in the project like a family. And

if they've got good ideas, take 'em. Anyone who resists other people's ideas is a fool.

I rarely improvise. It's all in the preparation. You need to work on the script and work on the script and work on the script until it's foolproof. Then be prepared to be absolutely dogmatic that's what you want to do. But also be prepared to change at the last moment.

That's how I work on feature films and commercials. Meticulous, regimented preparation, like a military operation. British Airways 'Globe' was the easiest, most relaxed commercial I've ever made. We knew exactly what we were going to do. We rehearsed and rehearsed the group of children. Then it was just a matter of turning up with a helicopter and shooting it.

If you don't pay attention to the fact that you are making the film to sell a product, you're absolutely irresponsible and the film will fail since it

has no logic. The product should infiltrate every pore and frame of a commercial and in all cases lead to its climax. Think about Ridley Scott's Hovis film. The boy climbing the hill with a pannier on the front of his bicycle, delivering bread. The bread is constantly apparent. When I did the Benson & Hedges film with the iguana, the fantasy needed some reality. I added the last shot of two people walking past a hoarding which told you what the film was about because I felt you needed to see the product at the climax.

For Dubonnet, we did a series of tableaux that were like reproductions of impressionist paintings. I copied Renoir and Manet. No doubt people copy my work. Advertising is plagiarism. Making a good commercial is the ultimate cliché. It's making cliché not seem like cliché. Don't try to pretend it's art.

I made my first commercial in 1964. I still enjoy it. I hope I'm still doing it when I'm 64.

Hugh Hudson

Courage Best 'Gertcha'
1979 and 1992

Out of retirement came Robert Krasker famed cinematographer ('El Cid', 'The Third Man') to create the special visual one take style for this witty and effective John Webster script. One of the most popular commercials of the seventies.

Cinzano 'Airplane'
1980

A classic comedy script from CDP. One of a series made with Joan Collins and Leonard Rossiter. Sharp and succinct, Rossiter's comic genius is an example of the seventies style of sit-com anecdotal commercial.

Agency
BMP

Photography
Robert Krasker

Music
Chas & Dave

Script
John Webster

Director/Producer
Hugh Hudson

Agency
Collett Dickenson Pearce

Photography
John Alcott

Actors
Joan Collins
Leonard Rossiter

Director/Producer
Hugh Hudson

Benson & Hedges 'Iguana'
1983
Alan Waldie's greatest moment... The wit and
surrealism of Waldie meets the visual style and poetry
of Hugh Hudson's camera. In one of Collett's greatest
spots. A mythical advertising film and a style of epic
production out of fashion in the 90s. One of the all
time greats of British advertising.

Agency
Collett Dickenson Pearce

Photography
Peter Suschitzky

Music
10CC

Script
Alan Waldie

Director/Producer
Hugh Hudson

Hugh Hudson

Handbuilt by Robots   **Poem**

Fiat Strada 'Handbuilt by Robots'
1983
Famous music again, Rossini 'Figaro' and Vangelis. The film was initially released in a 90-second version. Frank Lowe buying a whole commercial break to launch the film. The shooting was held up for five days owing to industrial action at Fiat in Turin, an ironic situation since there's no labour shown in the film itself. Paul Weiland was the copywriter – however only one copyline appears on the film – 'Handbuilt by Robots'!

British Rail 'Poem'
1988
Pastiche at its best. W.H. Auden's aped copy spoken by Tom Courtenay. The British Rail Network finally gets class. The film was a pre-privatisation boost with its beautiful sweeping aerial views of Britain shot from Mark Wolff's helicopter. And perfectly married with a hymn from Vangelis.

Agency
Lowe Howard-Spink

Agency
Lowe Howard-Spink

Music
Rossini/Vangelis

Music
Vangelis

Photography
John Alcott

Photography
Juan Ruiz Ancia

Script
Paul Weiland

Aerial
Mark Wolff

Editor
Pam Power

Director/Producer
Hugh Hudson

Director/Producer
Hugh Hudson

Genius **Global Face**

Guinness 'Genius'
1993
A seamless voyage though the black velvet
...wonderful art direction from Assheton Gorton
using almost every technique, model false perspective,
painted perspective, miniatures, CGI, green screen,
motion control, live action, 3-dimension hot-head,
dialogue, slow motion. Rutger Hauer stars as the man
in black.

British Airways 'Global Face'
1989
The face of the world's favourite airline. A thousand
teenagers, choreographed by Olympic designer Judy
Cipolla, make up the Picasso nose, ears, eyes and
mouth. Filmed through Utah's canyons and deserts.
Lakmé's beautiful aria completes this minimalistic
gem.

Agency
Ogilvy & Mather

Agency
Saatchi & Saatchi

Art Director
Assheton Gorton

Director/Producer
Hugh Hudson

Photography
Peter Suschitzky

Music
Brian Eno

Director/Producer
Hugh Hudson

 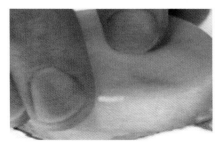

Klein

A talented commercial artist and illustrator, Daniel Kleinman began his career designing storyboards for music videos after graduating with a first-class degree in graphic design. He became a director in 1983, shooting over 100 promos for artists as diverse as Madonna, Prince, Heaven 17 and Fleetwood Mac. He pioneered the use of video effects and was soon in demand from advertising agencies, shooting scripts for Coca-Cola, Taunton Cider and Camel Cigarettes. More recent commercials like Audi A3 'Gauntlet', VW 'Test Track', Boddingtons 'Mansion' and GGT's John Smith's Extra Smooth campaign starring Jack Dee epitomise his ability to blend comic observation with post production wizardry. Kleinman's television credits include the spoof documentary 'Smashie & Nicie – The End of an Era' which won the Silver Rose Best Comedy award at the Montreux Television Festival. In 1995 Eon Productions invited him to direct the title sequence for the James Bond film 'Goldeneye'.

The most important thing is the idea. Everything I do is idea-based which gives me the potential to do something new. I don't particularly look for a script to be funny or beautiful, so long as I know that I would enjoy watching it myself.

Sometimes a script with a good idea is over-written so its potential is difficult to spot. Seeing that potential in what may otherwise not appear promising comes with experience. As long as you don't lose sight of what the agency is trying to get at, you can develop the script and push away parts you don't like. I don't take scripts as verbatim and I think a lot of creatives want you to have input. Or I hope they do. They get mine anyway.

Making a commercial has to be a collaborative process and I feel unhappy if I'm expected just to follow the orders of the agency. That's completely pointless. They might as well just get a DOP and do it themselves. Conversely, I don't like working entirely in isolation. I actually enjoy hearing other

opinions, as long as I feel that finally there's only one director: me. One of the agency's roles is to keep a distance between me and the client. Obviously I want to be friendly, but the agency have account managers to make sure clients understand what's going on.

Whenever I do storyboards I usually draw them myself and develop the script myself and get references together – so I can broaden it out. Even the simplest ideas can be interpreted in many ways. As a director, you are employed for your particular interpretation. All I do is have an opinion, I don't physically do anything: I don't work the camera, I just sit in a chair and talk.

I feel technique should be subservient to the idea. There are some directors who do things the other way round. They've got a certain style and the ideas always have to fit, whereas I prefer to match the idea with the most relevant style which means every project is slightly different. Because I've got experi-

ence of many different disciplines and techniques I can work in whatever style I feel is appropriate. I like that challenge. It's part of what makes commercials so interesting. My background in music videos has proved very useful. Promos are a great way to experiment. I use my illustrative experience to sketch out ideas. And I still use painting a lot as reference.

Because commercials are so condensed, every minute detail counts. Drawing things in advance helps me build up a narrative picture, so that I can see pictorially how everything is working. Although nowadays I don't show people storyboards that are too beautifully drawn and detailed, especially if I haven't done them myself. It fixes a preconceived picture too firmly in everyone's mind. *I* create the shots and action – not the storyboard artist.

I like working in an environment where everybody is motivated. I prefer encouragement to intimidation. If everybody is angry at each other or there's politics going on, that's when I stop being able to concentrate on work properly – which is why I always try to keep a good atmosphere. It's not my style to stomp and scream. I save that for when I'm at home with the wife.

I don't think there's too much emphasis placed on the director's role. It can be a very difficult job, particularly when you have to bring a complex idea to life. There's a big gap between interpretation and realisation. You need to have the director there to focus everybody's creative attention. Most people who work on an ad, from the costume designer to the art director, work in a certain amount of isolation. Their number-one priority is to do their bit absolutely right. They should be aware of what everybody else is doing to a certain extent, but it's unreasonable to expect them to be able to know everything, so you need one person who has got that overview, who can make sure that all the individuals are working towards the same goal.

I'm good at getting a clear idea of how something should look, including what alternatives and options are needed to enable editing to be properly part of the creative process.

Probably your most valuable asset is time, and new technology can be good for saving time, but I don't like technology for its own sake – even though I'm known for special effects work. Every script and every shot should be telling a story. If you're just looking at an effect, you're making a mistake.

I think advertising has gone through different fashions but I don't think it's intrinsically changed. Ever since I've been shooting commercials, it's always seemed that the best ads are trying to push the boundaries of what has been done before. Creatives have always tried to be innovative and I don't think that's changed. I think people still want to make great ads.

My advice to prospective directors is always to work with people who are better at their job than you are and stay away from the Craft Services table.

Boddington's Manchester Gold 'Mansion'
1996
Here I wanted to make stunning images that push pretentiousness to the edge of credulity without revealing the parody. It's amazing how far you can push it. I'm not sure some of the male models ever realised. However taking it too far would have defused the woman's joke and performance. If an actor doesn't want to put a slightly decomposing fish on his head, stand your ground.

Volkswagen Passat 'Test Track'
1997
The photographic style I chose for this was 'action movie', as the idea, a study in obsession, was basically narrative. There were lots of elements to juggle, characters, humour, action and ..er..oh...yes, the car driven very fast by a precision stunt driver. He only made one mistake during filming. On his final shot he was meant to drive towards us and stop before he hit anything. His parting words were ones you don't really want to hear – "sorry about the camera". The crash dummy baby became an essential finale but it was one of several extra gags kept in my back pocket.

Director
Daniel Kleinman

Producer
David Boterell

Production Company
Limelight

Lighting Camerman
Harris Savides

Editor
Steve Gandolfi

Agency
Bartle Bogle Hegarty

Copywriter
Jo Moore

Art Director
Simon Robinson

Agency Producer
Frances Royle

Director
Daniel Kleinman

Producer
David Botterell

Production Company
Limelight

Lighting Camerman
Ivan Bird

Editor
Steve Gandolfi

Agency
BMP DDB

Copywriters
Nick Gill,
Andy Mcleod

Art Director
Richard Flintham

Head of Television
Howard Spivey

National Dairy Council 'Floppy'
1995
The scripts for this campaign were mostly dialogue, so I added lots of visual gags. One of my favourite things is mild concussion so I created a little ballet of head bangs. It was important that after hitting himself once, Paul congratulated himself for side-stepping the next lamp-post before banging into the third. We made up and tried a lot of ideas as we went along which gives a very fresh spontaneous feel. It also meant we ended up with 8 films having started only making 5. I still got paid the same though.

UK Gold 'Mansworld'
1996
Oddly it's quite difficult to make something look crap. It's down to styling, performance and lighting, all of which have to be good to be bad in the right way. Doing something like this every now and then is a tonic to the endless pursuit of the beautiful. When the two men's suits dissolve away to leave them drinking in their underwear it wasn't really necessary to have a third man enter in his Y-fronts, but it made me laugh.

Director
Daniel Kleinman

Producer
David Botterell

Production Company
Limelight

Lighting Cameraman
Denis Crossan

Editor
David Yardley

Agency
BMP DDB

Copywriter
Dave Buchanan

Art Director
Mike Hannett

Agency Producers
Lucinda Ker
Frances Burke

Director
Daniel Kleinman

Producer
David Botterell

Production Company
Limelight

Lighting Cameraman
John Mathieson

Editor
David Yardley

Agency
GGT

Creative Directors
Robert Saville
Jay Pond-Jones

Copywriter
Alan Moseley

Art Director
Graham Cappi

Agency Producer
Katy Boyles

Daniel Kleinman

Camel 'A Matter of Taste'
1994
I like these ads because they are very simple. They had lots of large Germans rolling about in the aisles in German cinemas – no mean feat. The technology is already out of date and very primitive but it doesn't matter. The idea is the important thing, and the character one can put into a piece of fur and rubber. The puerile among us will still find these funny in a hundred years.

Audi A3 'Gauntlet'
1996
One could take the sting in the tail of this ad away and be left with a set of extraordinary images that stand up in their own right. The effects though are still subservient to the idea. Location was key to the mood and epic nature, although a lot was done in the edit. This is a loud big screen TV ad. I love it.

Director
Daniel Kleinman

Producer
Siobhan Barron

Production Company
Limelight

Lighting Cameraman
Clive Tickner

Editor
David Yardley

Agency
McCann-Erickson, Frankfurt

Director
Daniel Kleinman

Producer
David Botterell

Production Company
Limelight

Lighting Cameraman
Ivan Bird

Editor
Steve Gandolfi

Flame
Tom Sparks

Agency
Bartle Bogle Hegarty

Copywriter
Roger Beckett

Art Director
Andy Smart

Agency Producer
Frances Royle

**John Smith's Extra Smooth
'Jeopardy' and 'Glamour'**
1996
The most difficult thing here was to get across visually that Jack Dee was really in the situation you see him in but also make people aware that actually he's not, and of course he doesn't know where he is at all. Both ads use the same takes of Jack so the penguin action had to be worked out carefully to fit him, this still left room for some spontaneity. Jack going up a penguin's bum was quite a late addition. A real case of idea and technique working hand in hand as they should.

Director
Daniel Kleinman

Producer
David Botterell

Production Company
Limelight

Lighting Cameraman
Denis Crossan

Editor
Steve Gandolfi

Effects Editors
Tim Webber
David Yardley

Agency
GGT

Writers
Robert Saville
Jack Dee

Art Director
Jay Pond-Jones

Agency Producer
Diane Croll

Ian McMillan began his career in 1955 at Technicolor before becoming a camera assistant. Since 1964, he has worked as a director of photography on commercials, features, concert films and documentaries. After making several short films for cinema and television, he joined Park Village as a commercials director in 1982. His work for John Smith's bitter won a Gold at Cannes and Silver at D&AD in 1982. British Rail 'French Connection' won a Clio in New York in 1987 and his commercial for Vim has won five awards across Europe.

I'm a craft-based director. I began in feature films in the 60s, working my way up through the camera department. By the time I was operating and lighting, commercials had evolved into a sophisticated industry. It provided me as a cameraman with a great opportunity to learn my craft and play with the toys – to hire the very latest equipment and work on some spectacular shots. I enjoy the craft, but I also love working with actors; so I suppose I approach directing from both ends.

The kind of scripts I wanted to do and was lucky enough to get were light comedies. They were little stories, miniature films. I liked it when I could contribute something to the idea, but when you're working with someone like John Webster who's quite brilliant, you couldn't begin to suggest anything better than what was in the script. My job was to make the script work on film.

Even if you can't draw (like me), I think it's a good thing to storyboard. It concentrates your mind on how you're going to make the story work in the given time. Quite often, you'll discover it's running over by ten seconds. Sometimes you need to do more than storyboard to get the timing right. When I did the British Rail 'Coronation Scot' film which was effectively one helicopter shot of an InterCity train overtaking the Flying Scotsman, I was very concerned we might not be able to do it all in the time. So I got some model trains and filmed them in a studio to be sure it would work.

The storyboard also makes you condense all the information you want to get into the film and forces you to work out your lefts and rights. It makes you think about what size and angle you want. It takes me hours and hours, and I'll keep rubbing out what I've done and starting again. But by the time it's done, I do know the script inside out. On set, I'll give the storyboard to the rest of the crew. It helps to

ensure that everyone on set knows what's being done that day.

I enjoy both studio and location shooting. Each requires a completely different attitude. In a studio, you have complete control – you don't have to worry about the sun going in or out. You can organise the perfect composition, the best lighting and do as many takes as necessary. On location, you don't have such luxuries, but you can go to places which you could never recreate in the studio and shoot a wonderful landscape at exactly the right time of day.

A set works from the top down. How the director behaves affects how everybody else behaves, so I try to keep my shoots calm and workmanlike. Sometimes, I've wondered whether if I rant and rave, maybe we'd get on a bit quicker – but it's not really me. I like everybody to feel happy and relaxed on the set. If the actors are trying to get a performance right and they sense tension in the air, I don't think it helps

them. Some directors regard actors as no more than a necessary evil, but I feel you should really take care of them. It's a very vulnerable job, so if you give them a lot of encouragement, you'll get more out of them.

The better the actor, the less you need to do as a director. I prefer to give an actor free rein, but the trouble with commercials is that so much depends on the timing. Very often you have to ask an actor to condense what they're doing – make them do the laugh and the look simultaneously rather than one after the other.

Apart from making the story work, I think the director's job is also to create the atmosphere in which a magical moment can happen. When you think of film, you think of great images – King Kong and Faye Wray on top of the Empire State building, or Marilyn Monroe's skirt lifting up, or Humphrey Bogart in the mist at the end of 'Casablanca'. I worked with a choreographer on a couple of com-

mercials and I was very struck by the way that at certain moments in the routine, he'd get the dancers to make a very strong composition. "Make a picture," he would say. That's what you're aiming for as a director. You can't always plan it. When I shot John Smith's 'Dog', I remember looking through the viewfinder and seeing the dog sitting on the very tatty sofa. It was a perfect image. On the Mintoes 'Driving Lesson' film, the magic moment was supplied by the hilarious expression on the face of the actor playing the learner driver. I couldn't take any credit for that – it was just a moment in which everything in the story seemed to gel around what the actor did.

My career as a director has been affected by the arrival of new technology and the new generation of directors who've grown up around it. The commercials I liked to do have gone out of fashion. I'm not sad about it. Things have to change, new styles have to be allowed to evolve.

Ian McMillan

Dog

Signal Box

John Smith's 'Dog'
1981

The best thing that ever happened to me in my career was that John Webster gave me some scripts to shoot, and this was the most successful commercial I ever made.

Here are some of my early sketches. Luckily I quickly saw that it was best to shoot with the dog the other side of the bar.

In the end it was a simple 'split-screen' job, the actors having to do a complete take to fit within 30 seconds, while imagining the dog's actions in between them. We spent the rest of the day, and some of the next, shooting all the cuts of the dog to fill the centre of the panel. We made the mistake of sending the rushes to the lab on two different nights and so we never could get the colour of the middle panel the same all the way through.

There were many dog casting sessions, I must have seen nearly two hundred dogs, including circus acts, but there was only one that made me laugh just to look at it.

Yellow Pages 'Signal Box'
1985

Working with children is either a joy or a long uphill struggle. How can you argue when the star says "I don't want to do it again, filming is boring". But if kids like acting and are interested in filming then they are the most co-operative of all. You just need plenty of time (but hardly ever get it) to find them.

Darren Harris knew exactly what was wanted and gave a good performance every time.

Copywriter/Art Director
John Webster

DOP
Peter Jessop

Film Art Director
Tony Noble

Editor
Simon Cheek

Copywriter
Derek Day

Art Director
Andy Airghyrou

DOP
Pete Jessop

Film Art Director
Roger Burridge

Editor
Pam Power

Instructor

Marinero

Nuttals Mintoes 'Instructor'
1988
This was a low budget film so we had to shoot quickly and work out how to make it without damaging any cars.

Luckily I had two very good actors, Perry Benson and Bill Thomas. I have worked with Perry four times now and on this one he was brilliant.

Vim 'Marinero'
1989
This was a commercial that got better and better as we made it. The basic story was that a sailor arrives to start a new job, finds the ship's galley filthy and cleans it up. Martin Johnson built an excellent set, John Fenner lit it beautifully, the agency chose some unusual music, Louis Armstrong singing 'Peanut Vendor' which worked perfectly, and the actor really got into the part, even doing a little dance to the music. And you can always find a good composition with boats, trains or farmyards.

Copywriter
Tony Malcolm

Art Director
Guy Moore

DOP
Ian McMillan

Editor
Brian Dyke

Copywriter
Luis Perez Solero

Art Director
Fernando Villar

DOP
John Fenner

Film Art Director
Martin Johnson

Editor
Brian Dyke

Ian McMillan

Snowstorm

French Lessons

Standard Fireworks 'Snowstorm'
1986
This was an extremely low-budget commercial, but such an interesting idea that we subsidised it.

Filming in a real Dakota at Duxford Air Museum we tried to imitate a 50s film look and include all the stock characters in a disaster movie.

John Smith's 'French Lessons'
1981
I thought I would choose some lesser-known commercials for the showreel, to make it more interesting, and everyone has seen the 'Dog' anyway.

This one shot film shows that with a good script and some good actors you don't need much more.

I loved working with Gordon Rollings and Charles Pemberton and here they acted together beautifully. Gordon was an extremely talented comedian, sadly under-used in his too brief life.

Agency Producer
Richard Pilkington

DOP
Gerry Turpin

Editor
Brian Dyke

Copywriter/Art Director
John Webster

DOP
Peter Jessop

Art Director
Tony Noble

Editor
Simon Cheek

British Rail 'Imposing Trains'
1986
Now the most complicated commercial I ever made. The brief was 'a 50-second montage in the style of an American feature'. I had already made a ten-minute film with two superimposed images throughout, so I knew some of the problems. There were eight shooting days, including two days in a helicopter, with a second crew on the ground. I decided to do the helicopter filming myself, because communication is difficult in the air, and it is easier to shoot first and analyse later, before the shot, and the train, have gone.

Then, after drawing all the shots on paper and spreading them out all over the video house floor, with lots of help from Pam Power this was the result.

Sports Aid 'Military Spending'
1986
In 1986 I was very pleased to shoot two commercials for Sports Aid. Although 'Child' had more exposure at the time I've included this one because it's the most important message I've ever worked on, as applicable to the world today as it was then.

Voice-over
(Alan Bates): "Today, like every other day the world's military forces will blow 3 billion pounds on arms. Today, like every other day 14,000 children will die from malnutrition and disease."

Copywriter
Richard Phillips

Art Director
Ann Carlton

DOP
Freddie Young

Editor
Pam Power

Copywriter
Alex Ayuli

Art Director
Anita Davis

Editor

DOP
Ian McMillan

Mora

After studying graphics and film in London and producing for directing team Morton/Jankel, Andy Morahan began a distinguished career as a director of music videos, working with top artists such as George Michael, Elton John, Tina Turner, Paul McCartney, Van Halen and Guns n' Roses. In 1994, he directed the action thriller, 'Highlander III', before teaming up with producer Laura Gregory at Great Guns and launching himself as a commercials director. His first major commercial was 'Cheat' for Guess Jeans, starring Harry Dean Stanton and Juliette Lewis. It won over 60 awards including four D&AD Silvers and six Clios. Apart from his work in commercials, Andy also recently directed 'Murder In Mind', an independent feature, and executive-produced 'Push', the pilot for a US network drama series with ABC.

Having spent 12 years making music videos, I was in danger of becoming the director in 'Spinal Tap'. The last straw was going to Minneapolis for a meeting with Axel Rose. Two and a half weeks later, I'm on tour with the band, still trying to have the meeting... That's when I knew it was time to get out.

As a promo director, I had never been into post production wizardry. I have a low boredom threshold. Sitting in front of Harry for weeks on end isn't my idea of fun. I always had a cinematic intention (or pretension); I was 'Mr Narrative' – I tried to work a story into every concept. Crossing over to commercials, I was lucky with Guess? 'Cheat'. For me, it was the right product with the right people at the right time. Paul Marciano allowed us incredible freedom, so I was able to design and shoot a piece of work that was totally in line with my style and the kind of films I wanted to make. However, I was a little nervous when we did it because it did not seem like an ad at all – and I wondered if I was going too far. Advertising had been through the super-visual late-80s/early-90s, and I think there was a kind of undercurrent of desire to return to a more classic,

dialogue-based kind of film-making. So 'Cheat' seemed to fulfil that and, as a knock-on, a whole new career for me in advertising.

I think that ad people – especially in the UK – expect the director to become a really integral part of the creative team these days. A whole new generation of directors has come through recently and has helped to dissipate the lingering 'them and us' thing that existed between agencies and production companies in the 80s; it has really loosened up. The days of excess and mistrust have disappeared and the emphasis now is on creative collaboration.

I've never shot a script without trying to find a way of enhancing it, making it better – and most of the people I work with are responsive to that. I never storyboard stuff that tightly. I'll just draw up the key frames. Initially I'll shoot the material as per the script – but this is just a solid base to expand and springboard from. I'm always looking to find other ways of exploring the idea and trying to improve it. When I did Kilkenny 'First Kiss', there were half a dozen specific scenes that were supposed to illustrate certain aspects of that experience. We wound up

shooting around eighteen; the idea and the fun we were having with it just seemed to grow. Also, this visual ad-libbing was directly in harmony with the improvisational nature of the narrative dialogue. The agency wanted to use Irish people cast off the streets; I was nervous initially – getting good stuff from non-professionals can be tough; but luckily, the Irish are such wonderful story-tellers. So we had no problem in that department. This approach is tough on production – the amount of footage can seem excessive but the results are worth it. I'm always looking for those 'moments'; trying to find that 'magic'.

My producer Laura Gregory and I have had a big crusade on casting since we made 'Cheat'. We try not to use the obvious casting agents who only do ads. We've made a big, big point of going to theatrical agents who've got interesting young actors, and checking out independent movies. Having gone through the feature film process a couple of times, I've learned the best way to work with actors is often not to try and control them; on occasion you have to let them off the leash. If something isn't working with an actor, I'm always trying to find

solutions, ways to relax them, or help them get the mood or the right energy. I may play a discordant piece of music on set to make them freaked out or edgy if that's how I need them to be. Or I'll encourage them to improvise to help them into character. On 'Cheat', Juliette Lewis was having real trouble getting into a scene one day, so I kicked everyone out of the room apart from me and the DOP. I began to ask her questions about the back story and her feelings about the character. She just started to play around and ad-lib, and suddenly me and the cameraman were like, "turn the camera this is fucking great". We could have cut a dozen things out of the material she gave us; as it happened we were able to use some of it as a 'teaser' that played alongside the 90-second commercial, which was a real bonus.

Interestingly, as I've become more experienced, I've got to be less of a control freak. I've really begun to enjoy the collaborative aspects of film-making. Time was when I'd only use one or two cameramen because I was thinking, I can't afford to fuck this job up. Now I've got the confidence to go out and work with people who I may not know but whose work I

really admire, and let them do their own thing. Delegation and trust are really important – you can't do everything yourself. Same with editors. I never used to allow them to make a single edit if I wasn't in the room; now I've learned to sit back, let them do a first cut to see what they can bring to the party. I try not to have too preconceived ideas. When John Smith cut 'Cheat', he gave me this very montage-y approach which was just fantastic. He did it again on 'Barclays'. If you're able to work with talented people, they'll help you make a quantum leap with the footage.

A few things I've learned:

Do your homework. You can't take a meeting if you haven't really thought about it and prepared what you want to do.

If you believe in something, fight your corner. Otherwise you can't sit there and complain about it afterwards when it doesn't turn out how you wanted.

Throw off the shackles of caution and fear and throw yourself into the process. You can't make a film with blinkers on.

Guess? Jeans 'Cheat'
1996

This was an extraordinary job which launched my career in commercials. I was approached by producer Laura Gregory (Great Guns), a long-term friend and associate, with a loose idea for a 'Guess?' commercial that she had been asked to commission directly by the client, Paul Marciano. In the absence of an 'ad agency' she had Paul Shearer and Rob Jack (then at Simons Palmer, now at BBH) formulate a script that became the basis of the subsequent spot. Featuring the narrative voice of a insalubrious L.A. private-eye who specialises in 'decoy entrapment' the idea evolved and expanded to become a contemporary, 90s, black and white film noir that was more cinematic than advertising in its approach.

There were a number of reasons that contributed to this:
i) the original brief was for theatre/cinema/cable TV showings only, in a 90-second format.
ii) the client's desire to further reflect the inherent, classic film, 'Hollywood' glamour-influenced print campaigns that 'Guess?' had become known for.
iii) the casting of 'name' actors in the principal roles to give it a 'movie' credibility and to make it more of an 'event' than just another 'jeans' commercial in the overcrowded market place.
iv) the total creative freedom entrusted to us by the client that further encouraged us to be different and experimental.

Quite incredibly we attracted a cast that was beyond our wildest dreams. Harry Dean Stanton, Juliette Lewis, Traci Lords and Peter Horton.

From the first showing the commercial had the most amazing reaction. It was run all over the world and went on to receive over 60 different awards worldwide, and was voted the 'top commercial' in the US in 1996.

Bacardi 'Leaving'
1996

This was an interesting project. It was the second phase of a campaign which had originated the year before with two commercials featuring the same roguish D.J. character. The basic themes were also similar – i.e. the words he was broadcasting had a double meaning to those in the know. The basic difference (apart from the story-line obviously) was on this one the agency and the client really wanted to establish where this was taking place. The other spots had been shot in a dark and moody way (at night) and there was a feeling that they lacked a sense of geography and location. As a result, a more daylight approach was required, which meant we had to find one place that not only reflected and maintained the desired Latin/Caribbean/South American feel, but had a variety of locations to match the narrative of the script. This was much harder than we originally anticipated and after a long and arduous search (that included just missing the hurricane devastation in Puerto Rico) we found the most beautiful working fishing village called Alvarado, which was south of Veracruz on the Gulf Coast of Mexico. It proved to be ideal.

Barclays 'Voucher'
1997

'Voucher' was one of three promotional films (not commercials as such, in all but name) that I shot for JWT as part of their campaign for 'Barclays' newly acquired sponsorship of cinema in the U.K. As a strategy, they'd devised three films that were conceived and designed to be like movie trailers: none of them were supposed to be specific parodies as such but they had to be in 'the style' of what is a recognisable form. The basis of this idea was to run them in and amongst the 'real' thing, so the key or the trick if you like, was to make them as indistinguishable from the trailers as possible. We had to make people believe that these were for 'real' films and only reveal them as 'ads' at the very end. This threw up a number of different problems that had to be solved and out of the three, 'Voucher' was probably the hardest to pull off.

Conceived in the genre of a big spectacular action thriller it had to compete in terms of production with what one has come to expect from a contemporary 'Hollywood', 'event' movie. On top of this we had to create a sense of drama, excitement and interest around what in effect was a non-existent film. All this without even the advantage of recognisable 'stars' or the solid narrative of a 'real' film to fall back on.

However, after studying hundreds of trailers we realised that we had one thing really going for us; most of them are random combinations of unrelated yet extremely impactful and often spectacular visuals that have been thrown together to generate the maximum amount of interest and adrenaline-pumping excitement. In fact they don't want to give the story away at all, so they usually add a deep melodramatic voice that may give you a vague clue (if you're lucky) to the 'matter of life and death' 'high stakes' at hand, combined with a fast moving, quick cut, friendly piece of deliberately over-dramatic music. This may sound like a cynical over-simplification but it is really not. The realisation of this was actually the key that unlocked the whole creative process and determined the look and style of the subsequent film. The non-linear, non-narrative form actually allowed us to have more fun with the concept and visuals, giving us the freedom to throw in those 'random', unconnected, yet exciting shots. Also the double-edged beauty of this was it allowed us to allude to a bigger, wider story (the fictitious film) which further enhanced the deceit we were trying to pull off. A good example of this is the opening shot: a fast push into a black, unmarked security van whose doors burst open to reveal a heavily armed, trigger-happy, S.W.A.T. team, leaping out into the street ready for action. On its own it means nothing, but it immediately tells the audience that there is a 'situation' and it's primed to go off. It also lets us know it's an 'action' genre which we maintain and follow up with epic scale explosions towards the end.

We further enhanced our 'trick' by setting it in an American city (more believable as a backdrop) and casting almost familiar, usually B role, supporting actors that crop up regularly in good movies and drama series television. This gave it an immediate credibility. By all accounts and feedback, it worked a treat.

Barclays 'Boy Meets Girl'
1997

This was part of the same campaign but based on a whole different genre – the romantic comedy, mixed with a bit of 'coming of age', teenage angst. A classic movie theme that people like John Hughes have been plundering for years. Again the style was advantageous in helping us allude to a bigger, wider story but there was one element that was completely different to 'Voucher' in this respect. In that film the characters were just players in a tension-building, ticking-clock, time-bomb drama with the future of the 'world' at stake. In 'Boy Meets Girl' we realised that it was an altogether more human story and in the absence of a 'real' story we had to care about these people. This resulted in us becoming less non-linear and actually restoring more of a narrative format than was originally intended. In effect we had to resolve certain things that actually most trailers try to avoid. They like to keep the audience hanging in a state of unfulfilled limbo, intrigued but hungry for more. In this film the convention was perpetuated for as long as possible but ultimately felt better with a sense of fulfilment. Ironically this became more of a short movie than a 'fake' trailer but weirdly enough nobody seemed to be unduly bothered by this.

On reflection I think that there were some inherent factors within the script that really contributed to this and which turned out to be first-class ideas. The concept of the boy and girl coming from totally opposite sides of the track, from different social and financial worlds, made the likelihood of them coming together virtually impossible. The odds were stacked against them; but herein lies the essence of romance; like two comets colliding in the heavens, their fate was sealed. This was the key; everybody connects with this; we're all searching and yearning for the purity and magic of the perfect love; and in the face of adversity that is presented at the start, we immediately understand their predicament, invest emotionally in the characters and 'root' for the underdog in a defiant show of blind faith and support in the face of their unlikely triumph. This is why there had to be some resolution. If you care about the characters and their situation, you care about what happens to them. This made it very different from the other films but no less effective.

Evian 'Sugar Daddy'
1997
This was a very challenging project from a casting and budget perspective. It took so long to come to fruition that I'm surprised it actually happened at all. I was approached by Euro RSCG Wnek Gosper over a year before we shot it. I loved the script, despite being told the budget was really tight! It gave us the opportunity to cast an older character actor. We secured Lawrence Tierney (and Tully Jensen as his beautiful young wife), but sadly for us and Euro the French client just could not envisage Lawrence in the role of the rich older man and felt he was not the right image for the product. We finally cast a wonderful actor, Anthony Zerbe, for the lead and Gary Stretch for the scheming manservant. I had a lot of fun doing this job and really enjoyed exploring the comedy side of myself as a director.

Tia Maria 'Harry'
1996
There were two things about these films that really stick out for me. One was having to tell a narrative story in 20 seconds which required split-second timing and a level of disciplined film-making that I had not experienced before. Secondly this was a brand new campaign devised by Rainey Kelly Campbell Roalfe who had recently won the account on their creative pitch of a complete re-invention of the brand. In the past Tia Maria had always been associated with dark-eyed, dusky, exotic models like Iman. This time, although the client had conceptually bought into this change of direction, they found it very hard to approve any recommendations that were too far away from the comfort of their previous stereotypes. I remember their jaws dropping open when I suggested a girl with the most incredible blue eyes – Mizzi. However, this particular physical feature was a key element in the scripts, so we fought the battle, won it and the results speak for themselves. By the way, her eyes were so pale and photographically unusual it saved us a fortune in post production where we barely had to enhance them at all.

Renault Laguna 'Ginola Stays'
1996

This script was written as a specific, cinematic-style narrative featuring the French soccer star, David Ginola. Having become famous in the UK when he joined Newcastle FC, he was seen as part of the recent influx of foreign 'super-stars' who had been lured to the once-unfashionable, British Premier League by the over-inflated transfer fees and fat salaries. Suddenly every club was competing with each other to buy a 'dream team' and this was quickly and cynically exploited by greedy players who kept their options open by signing as short a contract as possible. As a result there was constant speculation about how long these players would stay at their 'new' clubs and the outrageous and tempting packages they were being offered by rival teams.

The script cleverly played on this and followed Ginola's secretive arrival in Italy via private jet in an effort to sign him to yet another lucrative contract by an anonymous, yet obviously successful and wealthy club. On the instruction of the team owner he's to be offered 'anything he wants' to make him sign. What follows is a montage of progressively more ridiculous temptations: from boats and houses to girls and gold bullion, we are drawn into an assumption that in the face of this seduction he can't possibly refuse; however the beauty of this 'distraction' is that it cleverly masks, yet sets up, the unexpected twist at the end. The car he is being driven around in is never featured or alluded to as anything other than a means of transport. So at the end when he 'signs', we pull out to reveal it is a cheque. He has bought the car, driving away to the astonishment of the bemused club officials. The conceit is beautiful and shows the strength of a well conceived and well structured script. Good narrative writing is rare in contemporary advertising, so this was very refreshing. Further bonus as a result was the way in which the story helped mask and protect Ginola's limited acting experience. The passivity of his role and the fact that he was playing himself allowed him to be natural, look cool and never expose his inexperience as an actor.

Another memorable plus of the shoot was the location of Naples and the stunning Amalfi coast as the back drop to the commercial. Shot by the Italian DOP Nicola Pecorini (camera-man to Bertolucci and Storaro) it gave the commercial an aesthetic sophistication and added an extra level of glamour to the overall theme of the 'temptation and seduction'.

VW Polo 'Surprise'
1996

This was a strange job because I came to it so late; the agency (BMP) had already committed to another director who had unexpectedly pulled out at the last minute. In a bit of a panic they came to me and although this was a situation that 99% of the time I would avoid there was something about the script that intrigued me and I felt I could really do something with it. Like 'Renault', I am attracted to the concept of car commercials that don't stuff the product down your throat. Most spots in this genre are all hard sell close-ups and driving shots of the vehicle. The attraction and difference on both of these projects were their conceptual basis in a more cinematic-style, narrative-driven structure. This allows the cars to become a subtle part of a bigger story-line along with the actors and the characters they play. This takes a lot of courage by the client because it is a huge step and usually against their natural instincts to play down the car but it is often very effective. I jump when I am given opportunities like this. It tests your craft as a story-teller and film-maker in the most classic sense and is part of my attempt to never rely on just being a visualist.

A final anecdote about this job was how I'm constantly amazed by the talent of great DOPs, not only was this beautifully shot by Daniel Pearl, the final shot of the car on the beach was shot in what, to the naked eye, seemed like total darkness. Pulling out all the filters and pushing the exposure two stops he shot it anyway. Privately, I was convinced it would have to be re-shot. I could not have been more wrong. It was great.

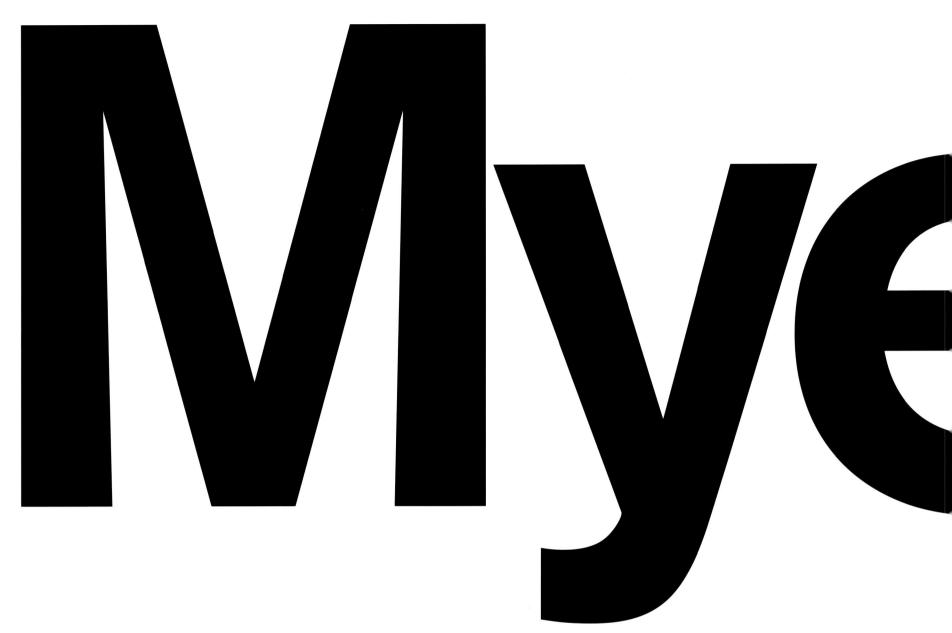

After working as a copywriter at FCB, Barry Myers joined Lintas where he worked exclusively on commercial scripts for three years. When he moved on to S.H. Benson's, he began producing and directing his own scripts. He then started his own company, Spots. During the subsequent 25 years of its existence, Spots grew to be one of the world's top production companies, with offices in the US and Paris, winning Golds in every major festival. Prizes at D&AD include several Pencils for Best Film and also one for Best Director. Barry now works through Jan Roy Associates in London and Rigaud Productions in Paris.

I love commercials. I love products. I can't bear it if a writer can't come up with a decent idea for Wall's ice-cream – something we were all brought up with. Products are a part of our lives. You can really use them to connect with people – to move them, or make them laugh. For me, a great spot is when you see a cracking story, a slice of human life – and it was all occasioned because of, for instance, the cigarette packet on the table in front of me.

Example: British Airways 'Boardroom'. Here's this back-stabbing group of 80s businessmen, and they've put their rival on the red-eye so he won't get any rest and will turn up too knackered to perform at the big meeting. So the whole spot hinges on this club-class ticket doing what they want it do. (It does not, of course.) Lynx 'Jealousy' – another great idea: the woman discovers her boyfriend is untrustworthy when she accidentally puts on his deodorant and immediately all these girls come on to her. Smirnoff 'People's Army': you drink the product and you no longer know if you're a peasant or an aristocrat.

Renault Clio 'Sicily' – the little Godfather looks over his new car and says, 'It's little, but it's big – just like me.' In all these spots, the product's the hero. The film wouldn't exist without it. If you can tell a story through the product, you'll really wow the audience – and you'll win all the prizes.

It's a big responsibility being a commercials director. You're at the sharp end of where the money is being spent. Campaigns now go all over Europe, all over the world. You often sit down for a car commercial and you may have representatives from ten countries and you have to listen to everybody, even if their needs are different from one another. There's so much riding on these spots. They cost so much money, they affect so many people in so many markets, so I think it's incredibly important to find out what the client wants. There's often some resistance among agencies to give the client what he wants, as if that's uncreative. But it isn't. Of course, it's easy to make a lousy common denominator film. The trick is to make a super spot that answers everyone's needs.

That's difficult and I think that requires experience.

I started as a writer in agencies. When I began directing, I had an agreement with a couple of agencies that if I wrote their material, they'd let me film it. That worked well, but the real test came when I had to learn to work for other writers. For me, everything starts with the script. Some creatives are rather surprised that I want to talk about the script more than the look, but I need to get the script as good as it can be before I get on to the film-making.

I never storyboard. This makes some clients and agencies incredibly worried, but how can you story-board your imagination? I can't. To me a film isn't prepared, it's discovered in the doing. The process of finding out how to tell a particular story is a continuous one. As soon as I set foot in a studio or on a location, I get turned on. I begin to get really excited about the story and the possibilities. I may only discover the key to the film when I'm doing a close-up on day two. I'll look through the viewfinder and there it is. Then I have to redo what I've done up to

that point, because now I've found out how to do it. It isn't logical, but that's how I work. I've made thousands of commercials like that. For example, when we did Smirnoff 'People's Army', we were on location in Hungary and I suddenly had the idea of cross-cutting between the revolutionaries and the aristocrat before they meet. That wasn't in the script, but it gave the film exactly the right rhythm and feeling. The idea was suggested to me by being in the location.

I usually shoot with two cameras and I operate one myself. If the set's looking good and the light-ing's beautiful, I just can't stop looking through the viewfinder (when I'm not on the camera, it won't be long before I'm having a word with the art director and the cameraman). I consider myself a good opera-tor. The trick is knowing what's wanted in the shot and seeing it happen. It's just like using your eyes. Some operators get obsessed with trying to get everything in the frame perfect – but it doesn't matter if the bloody tree on the edge of the frame wasn't in the shot or even if the boom was in –

what's important is that you get the action you wanted.

Casting is critical for me. Some people will say, "oh, he's not a good actor but you're a good director." Well, I can cut round him, I can encourage him but I can't really change what he's doing. So if I don't get it right in the casting, I've blown it. I'm in awe of good actors. If you really love and respect your cast, they'll give you everything they've got. Same with the crew. I used to terrorise agency people on set when they suggested something that didn't obey the laws of film, but never the crew – because they are film people through and through, and I have a fundamental love of technicians.

My joy has been learning film and learning how to tell stories. I get the feeling now that agencies know less and less about film. When I watch com-mercials, there's a lot of technique but not much film craft. And it shows up in the story-telling. It looks slick, it looks great – but if the story-telling was stronger, people would enjoy it more.

BA 'Boardroom'
1987
Made in the 80s, when greed was good! Businessmen wouldn't possibly do such things today, would they?

Smirnoff Black 'People's Army'
1995
The truth behind all revolutions: revolutionaries at first imprison, then are imprisoned in their turn.

Lynx 'Jealousy'
1996
What a product! One dab and the girls are all over you, even if you're a girl. My wife refuses to have it in the house.

Wright's Coal Tar Soap 'Macau'
1983
Only the Brits could produce a commercial for soap, where the main product benefit is that it will foil an assassination attempt.

Barry Myers

Superzoom   Sicily

Olympus 'Superzoom'
1988
The three rules behind any good film, writing, writing and writing.

Renault Clio 'Sicily'
1992
Shot in Sicily, but with New York actors. What a difference they made.

Department of Health 'Natural Born Smoker'
1985
I must have smoked more cigarettes on this shoot than on any other I can remember. I shot the film because I thought it would put off young smokers.

Louis Ng was born in the Portuguese colony of Macao and trained as an illustrator and graphic designer. He had every intention of becoming an agency art director but spotted a newspaper ad for a trainee at a Hong Kong commercials company. He spent the late 70s graduating from runner to assistant director before joining McCann-Erickson as a TV producer. In 1980 he started directing commercials. In 1983 he opened Film Factory with Lester Wong so that he could start directing the commercials he wanted, for the people he wanted. In 1989 he opened Film Factory Thailand in Bangkok with director Nang Siddhigu so that Nang could direct the commercials he wanted. In 1992 Louis opened Another Factory with Wilde Ng so that Wilde could direct the commercials he wanted.

Today, Louis has won too many awards and accolades to mention. He is universally regarded as Asia's best director – a title he never sought. All he wanted to do was shoot commercials.

A script is like a human being. When you meet, you listen to what he has to say, understand what he is trying to communicate and then decide whether you can have a worthwhile relationship.

I never demand freedom. Freedom implies that the agency's job is finished. I demand understanding. When we have understanding, we have trust and when we have trust we can start. Because once we start there is no turning back.

It sounds clichéd, but I always try to see myself as a consumer. I always ask myself if I look at my commercial, will I buy the product, do I believe or associate with the client? The irony is that the whole thing is a psychological game. A game that tries to capture a piece of the consumer's mind, evoking feelings for the clients and products we advertise. If it works, then the job is done and maybe I become a psychological criminal.

I am never attracted to ads in themselves, I'm attracted to the game. I enjoy the mind game we play with ads. Trying to understand how the consumer's mind works is the secret. If you get it right, you win. If you don't, you lose. Simple.

I prepare on three levels.

First, like a scientist. Look at the fundamentals, understand the basics and find the potential.

Second, like a film-maker. Finding a style and film language to communicate in.

Thirdly, like a game. Looking at the commercial in an objective and spontaneous way, so that it becomes something the audience and I enjoy playing.

I never do storyboards. I do a lot of thinking, writing, re-writing and re-writing on the mood, the tone and on the scenes. And even after I finish shooting, I keep playing until I find the simplest, most enjoyable way. To me there are only two things: thinking and fun.

I get my best results when I collaborate with agencies and clients who have vision. Without vision even the best director cannot perform at his best. Without vision the director is working on his own and it becomes masturbation.

Technology should be used as a tool, for example to perfect the images, to create scenes which can't be done normally. If you look at the great movies over the years – the ones that have left a lasting impression – you rarely find one where technology rules over art.

Technology has become such a trendy thing, so has advertising, so has directing. In the end, time will be the best judge.

Content is everything. If you have the best, directing is not important. Style and technology are not important. I originally came from advertising and as a result, I learnt the importance of content. Content always wins over beautiful executions. I always try to find a way to execute an idea in its most basic and simple form, in order to reveal the original content, whether it be art or stupidity, I always try to find images that have honesty.

Advertising is art with a motive.

Of course, as an art it keeps changing with the environment, with society, with the world. Is our world getting better or worse? Are our movies getting better or worse? Is our life getting better or worse? Is advertising getting better or worse? Maybe we should ask, "are our minds getting better or worse?"

What do I tell aspiring commercials directors?

Fuck the rules.

Be honest. Have fun.

Louis Ng

Marlboro 'CNY 97'   Hong Kong Tourist Association 'City of Dreams'
1997   1993

Director
Louis Ng

Art Director
Lai Pun Hang

Copywriters
Jet Lam
Fanny Chong

Creative Director
Jet Lam

Director of Photography
Lester Wong

Producer
May Tang

Agency
Leo Burnett

Agency Producer
Yvonne Ho

Production Company
The Film Factory, Hong Kong

Editor
Nelson Ng @ Touches, Hong Kong

Music
Musicad

Post Production Company
Touches, Hong Kong

Client
Phillip Morris Asia Inc

Director
Louis Ng

Art Director
Jon Slater

Copywriter
Michael Holt

Creative Directors
Michael Holt
Jon Slater

Director of Photography
Lester Wong

Producer
May Tang

Agency
Bozell

Agency Producer
Edith Cheung

Production Company
The Film Factory, Hong Kong

Editor
Nelson Ng @ Touches, Hong Kong

Music
Chong Wang

Post Production Company
Touches, Hong Kong

Client
Hong Kong Tourist Association

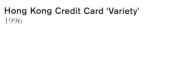

McDonald's 'Muki'
1993

Hong Kong Credit Card 'Variety'
1996

Director
Louis Ng

Art Director
Daren Spiller

Copywriter
David Alberts

Creative Directors
David Alberts
Daren Spiller

Director of Photography
Lester Wong

Producer
May Tang

Agency
DDB Needham

Agency Producer
Michael Ritchie

Production Company
The Film Factory, Hong Kong

Editor
Adrian Brady @ Touches, Hong Kong

Music
Musicad

Post Production Company
Touches, Hong Kong

Client
McDonald's

Director
Louis Ng

Art Director
Ron Cheung

Copywriter
Spencer Wong

Creative Directors
David Alberts
Spencer Wong
Ron Cheung

Director of Photography
Lester Wong

Producer
May Tang

Agency
Bates Hong Kong

Agency Producer
Rowena Chu

Production Company
The Film Factory, Hong Kong

Editor
Nelson Ng @ Touches, Hong Kong

Music
Musicad

Post Production Company
Touches, Hong Kong

Client
Hong Kong Bank

Corporate

Brother & Sister

KCRC 'Corporate'
1991

Optical 88 'Brother & Sister'
1994

Director
Louis Ng

Art Director
Joe So

Copywriters
K.C. Tsang
Catherine Kennedy

Creative Director
Ricardo de Carvalho

Director of Photography
Lester Wong

Producer
May Tang

Agency
Ogilvy & Mather

Agency Producer
Betty Tso

Production Company
The Film Factory, Hong Kong

Editor
Nelson Ng @ Touches, Hong Kong

Music
Schtung Music

Post Production Company
Touches, Hong Kong

Client
Kowloon Canton Railway Corporation

Director
Louis Ng

Art Directors
Paul Chan
Rachel Chau

Copywriters
K.C. Tsang
Angela Pong
Tony Wood

Creative Directors
K.C. Tsang
Paul Chan
C.C. Tang

Cameraman
Wicky Wong Kris Lo

Producer
May Tang

Agency
Ogilvy & Mather

Agency Producer
Betty Tso

Production Company
The Film Factory, Hong Kong

Editor
Nelson Ng @ Touches, Hong Kong

Music
Alvin Kwok

Post Production Company
Touches, Hong Kong

Client
Optical 88

Good Joss

Fisherman

Waste Management 'Good Joss'
1993

Hong Kong Bank 'Fisherman'
1995

Director
Louis Ng

Art Director
Dick Lemmon

Copywriter
Ron Hawkins

Creative Directors
Ron Hawkins
Dick Lemmon

Director of Photography
Lester Wong

Producer
May Tang

Agency
Ogilvy & Mather

Agency Producer
Monna O'Brien

Production Company
The Film Factory, Hong Kong

Editor
Adrian Brady @ Touches, Hong Kong

Post Production Company
Touches, Hong Kong

Client
Waste Management

Director
Louis Ng

Art Director
Rachel Chau

Copywriters
Angela Pong
David Alberts

Creative Director
David Alberts

Director of Photography
Lester Wong

Producer
May Tang

Agency
Bates, Hong Kong

Agency Producer
Rowena Chu

Production Company
The Film Factory, Hong Kong

Editor
Nelson Ng @ Touches, Hong Kong

Music
Chan Ming Cheung, Taiwan

Post Production Company
Touches, Hong Kong

Client
Hong Kong Bank

Noro

After completing the film course at the Royal College of Art in 1984, Mehdi Norowzian worked as an assistant director and continued to make his own short films with funding from the BFI. After being taken on as a director by the Redwing Film Company, who sponsored a further three shorts, his career as a commercials director took off. In 1994, Adidas 'FIFA' won him two Silvers at the British Television Awards. Later that year, he set up Joy Films with Desley Gregory, his former Redwing producer. His high-profile work has included films for Sony (nominated for direction by D&AD in 1996), Adidas, British Airways and his series for Mercury One 2 One featuring John McCarthy, Kate Moss and Vic Reeves – a campaign which won him a further two Silvers at the 1997 British Television Awards.

I never thought I'd fit into commercials. My background was a bit arty-farty. I'd made experimental films – upside-down, in negative, crazy things. I didn't know much about advertising. When I saw commercials on television or in the cinema, I'd think, wow, a lot of money's been spent on that. But they seemed so conservative, a world apart from the kind of films I was making. What interested me at the time was how to communicate without using words, how to express emotions and sensations visually, so you feel alienated, or secure, or joyful, or horny. I feel I achieved that goal – now I'm interested in continuing this process but also incorporating dialogue.

My first commercial was for Stella Dry. The creatives had written and recorded a voiceover and added music and sound effects to get a mood. They were prepared to let me do my own thing with the visuals. I didn't realise how unconventional this was at the time. I was just grateful to be doing it. But the commercial got an amazing response. It split people down the middle – they either hated it or loved it.

Some people were really offended – "this isn't a commercial – where's the idea?" But it was part of a change in advertising. Agencies and clients were reacting against tradition, and beginning to take risks with ideas and directors.

If the product is the driving force of a script, I'm not interested, to be honest. I'm not an advertising guru, but I think people are more interested in the attitudes or feelings associated with the product, rather than the product itself. That's why I enjoyed doing the Mercury 'One 2 One' films where the product is not an actual object but a whole service and name. Obviously, I'm happy to put the product in, but my advice to creatives is to think about the film first and foremost because that's what stays with you. And even if it only says 'Adidas' for two seconds at the end, that's enough. That was the film, now here's the product we're trying to sell you. I think that's an honest approach, and I think the audience appreciate it.

I won't just take someone's script and shoot it. I'll question it, play with it, offer you something new.

wzian

If you don't want that, there's no point coming to me. You're better off with a technician. I work best when the creatives give me a fair amount of freedom. When I did Adidas 'The Rock', I was given a script which said, 'Marcel Desailly trains with a demolition ball'. It was up to me to find the right situation, figure out how it would look and feel. And I was allowed to shoot it exactly the way I thought it should be, because the creatives trusted me. The problem with commercials sometimes is that there are too many people involved – too many ideas and opinions. It can be overwhelming and lead to compromise. If you can go with one vision, it may not always be right, but it will have clarity. So I think directors need to be really confident in the way they put over their vision.

Storyboarding is essential for me. I'm not the sort of guy who can go to Sainsbury's without a shopping list. Some things I can draw well, others I can't draw to save my life. So after I've sketched everything out, I bring in my storyboard artist and explain to him what I'm trying to achieve, say, a top

shot of Desailly with his back to the ball. When he's done it, I'll say, no, I want a wider shot. It's like working with a cameraman. It really makes me think what I'm going to shoot, and how I'm going to make it all fit together. You can have a wild idea, but if it doesn't work in the storyboard, you chuck it out. The storyboard becomes the blueprint for everything. It helps the agency and client to see what I'm going to do, so we can do all our fighting before the shoot. I used to produce, so for me the other advantage of storyboarding is that I'm better prepared for the shoot. I know what equipment I'm going to need, and how long for. Good economy allows you to be more creative, helps you get more production value.

I worked with performance artists a lot when I began making films. That got me very interested in the physical aspect of acting. Usually in commercials, you just see actors sitting there and talking. But they've got this incredible body and as a director, you should use it as ammunition – even if it's just in the way they walk across a room, or bump into an object. It's another layer you can use apart from dialogue.

When I was a film student at the Royal College of Art, fancy post production wasn't an option. I learned to do my effects in-camera using all the old, basic techniques. I love the clarity and integrity of that approach. Rather than shoot someone against chromakey blue for a 'flying' scene, I'll do it for real and use wires to suspend them on location – which is what I did for British Airways and Sony. If I can see it in front of camera, it's a real buzz. It means I get exactly the right feeling, and it looks perfect because everything's been shot in the same light. I never rely totally on post production – it feels like cheating.

I'm very hands-on in all aspects of production. I've built up a team around me and I welcome their input, but it has to be within certain parameters. It's up to me to initiate the idea and plant the same seed in everyone's minds. Whatever they suggest will then belong in the same film. If you don't do that, then collaboration can become a hindrance; everyone's opinions begin to conflict and you wind up saying "no" all the time rather than being creative.

Sony 'Road'
1995
I shot this commercial in the Salt Flats in Utah – a highway ran parallel to the Flats – and truck drivers kept reporting to the police that aliens had landed!

British Airways 'Business'
1996
The schedule on this was a nightmare, half the crew collapsed from exhaustion but it was great to work on something with such huge scale.

Client
Sony

Client
British Airways

Agency
BMP DDB Needham

Agency
M&C Saatchi

Art Director
Jerry Hollens

Art Director
Kevin Thomas

Writer
Mike Boles

Writer
Tony Barry

Stella Artois 'Filling'
1992
This was my first commercial – we shot it in Sydney – looking back on it I can't believe we had such an enormous amount of creative freedom.

Adidas 'The Rock'
1996
Desailly was an amazing athlete to work with. I hope the film reflects his amazing ability of movement and his grace.

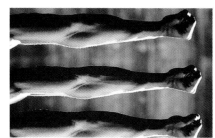

Client
Stella Artois

Agency
Lowe Howard-Spink

Art Director
Kevin Thomas

Writer
John Silver

Client
Adidas

Agency
Leagas Delaney

Art Director
Ian Ducker

Writer
Will Farquhar

One 2 One 'John 2 Yuri'
1996
Great Script, great team and great subject – John
McCarthy was an absolute inspiration. The film says
the rest.

Client
One 2 One

Agency
Bartle Bogle Hegarty

Art Director
Steve Hudson

Writer
Victoria Fallon-Butler

Joy – short film
1992
It's amazing what you can achieve in one afternoon on a Bolex with a talented friend. The result is pure joy (spirit).

Raised in London, Cumbria, Wales and Germany, Ridley Scott studied graphic design and painting at the West Hartlepool College of Art. He made his first short film at The Royal College of Art in London. During a travelling scholarship to the United States he worked with award-winning documentarians Richard Leacock and D.A. Pennebaker at Time Life Inc. Upon his return to England he joined the BBC as a production designer and became a director within a year. Three years later he formed RSA Films, now widely regarded as one of the world's most successful commercial production companies with offices in London, New York and Los Angeles. Scott began his feature directing career with 'The Duellists', which won him the Jury Prize at the 1978 Cannes Film Festival. His second film, 'Alien' won an Academy Award for Special Effects. Other credits include the landmark sci-fi thriller 'Bladerunner', 'Legend', 'Black Rain' and the Oscar-winning 'Thelma & Louise'. Since founding Scott Free with brother Tony, he has produced 'The Browning Version', produced and directed 'White Squall' and more recently completed 'G.I. Jane', starring Demi Moore.

Every director has a 'performance'. I always tell that to actors. By the time I start shooting, I've mentally built the sets, acted out the performances and already cut the film. I can see and hear the film in my head. Whether I'm making a commercial or a feature, content comes first and with that content comes the decision to get involved or not.

The first thing I do when I get a good script in is to draw storyboards. I can draw well. I spent enough time at art school, almost seven years! It's a bit like the writer with a blank page not knowing what to do. I will simply start with an empty sheet of paper and begin to doodle. Somewhere in the back of my mind is the 'vision' and so I start to draw, for inspiration and interpretation. This procedure can happen even before the job's been confirmed. Finding the 'vision' is very often the deciding factor:

whether to do it or not.

When I'm given a script, I invariably want to change it in some way. That's always the first discussion, with the creative group. It's vital to have an open dialogue immediately. Sometimes I win, sometimes I lose. If the agency wins, chances are they're right for their target. I'm not a prima donna, I'm very reasonable and a good listener. To lean too heavily on my own extensive experience makes for a very short life.

Young teams have to feel that the person they are dealing with is in touch. With my career both in films and commercials, 'been there, seen it and done it' can be the reason why I will turn something down. Unless I can find a fresh approach – 'the vision'.

I'm still enthusiastic about the commercial field

because the prolonged mental and physical process of making a feature is all-consuming. The pressure is enormous whereas, in a 40- or 60-second spot, the time involved is equally challenging but over a short space of time.

At the risk of sounding like an old codger, I don't think there are as many good ideas flying around now compared to 20 years ago. When I started 30 years ago, I was a visual director clamouring to get into the door of agencies like CDP and BMP because their work was 'dialogue and idea' driven. The direction has totally shifted because technology's become far more sophisticated and the marketplace has changed dramatically. We now have very visually driven ideas where the dialogue and emotion have gone out of commercials. Everyone talks in terms of high concept, high-tech, big sound, surreal

imagery. Love it! But there should be more of a mix, more considered copywriting and story-telling. Point of fact: huge success and reaction to the Guess? Jeans campaign in 1996! This film had everything a client and a production company (hungry for showreel material) could wish for. I've always loved the 'chase' and the competition in commercials and that's why I did hundreds, maybe thousands before I even thought of shooting a film. I loved it. I owe everything to commercials. There was no film school when I kicked off at art college and working in advertising was the first time I got my hands on celluloid and could make short movies.

I love the process of shooting – it's the preparation I don't like so much. Once I'm on set, that's where I get charged up. I'm nervous when the editing starts because, when you look at the first cut, it

always seems too slow or too this or that. Here, another challenge begins. Here, the story-telling really begins, the 'pacing', the creation of sounds and music to heighten the drama. This is my favourite part of the whole process.

How important is the director's role? Is it overemphasised? Actually, this a stupid question. It's like asking how important is the jockey on the horse. I don't think a director's role is overemphasised at all. The best directors give you a security in that they won't drop the ball, they'll add to the process, and the final product will hopefully be better than you expected. It's a double-edged question. There's a danger that experience can be regarded as a disadvantage, but, on the other hand, I think agencies generally get what they pay for – as long as they don't mistake 'hip' for 'hype'.

Apple Computer '1984'
1984

Gallager 'Border'
1972

Client
Apple Computer Inc

Client
Gallager Ltd

Director
Ridley Scott

Director
Ridley Scott

Production Company
RSA Films

Production Company
RSA Films

Producer
Nadia Owen

Lighting Cameraman
Peter Suschitzky

Set Designer
Mike Seymour

Agency
Collett Dickenson Pearce

Lighting Cameraman
Adrian Biddle

Agency Producer
Ray Barker

Editor
Pam Power

Art Director
Geoff Kirkland

Agency
Chiat/Day Inc Advertising, LA

Copywriter
Lindsay Dale

Agency Producer
Richard O'Neil

Advertising Manager
John Lake

Art Director
Brent Thomas

Copywriter
Steve Hayden

Marketing Director
Jean Richardson

Hovis 'Bike Ride'
1975

Client
Hovis Limited

Director
Ridley Scott

Production Company
RSA Films

Set Designer
Mike Seymour

Lighting Cameraman
Terry Bedford

Agency
Collet Dickenson Pearce

Agency Producer
Judy Hurst

Art Director
Ronnie Turner

Copywriter
David Brown

Marketing Director
Alan Hepburn

Sede

After graduating from the Art Institute of Chicago, Joe Sedelmaier spent the next ten years as an art director for Young and Rubicam and J. Walter Thompson in Chicago. During these years he wrote, directed and photographed two short films which won awards at the film festivals of Mannheim, London and San Francisco. In 1967 he started his own production company and began to build an international reputation for his highly-prized direction of humorous TV commercials for such clients as Federal Express, Mobil Oil, Alaska Airlines, U.S. Sprint and Wendy's. His numerous awards include countless Clios, a few Gold Lions, awards from the New York Art Directors Club and a D&AD Silver Pencil.

I'm often asked why I only do funny spots.

For me, humour has a way of keeping things in proportion; it's not creating this thing where one's saying, "hey, buy our toothpaste, perfume, shoes, whatever; you'll be more popular, happier, richer, and life will be more meaningful." I know this stuff sells but it's always made me squirm.

Besides, I've always loved comedy and anyone who could make me laugh. My heroes were Chaplin, Keaton, Fields, Laurel and Hardy.

But, when I began to direct the dominant notion in advertising was, "Humour doesn't work; you'll remember it's funny but you won't remember the product."

So, I mostly did 'serious' commercials that were funny – if not intentionally so.

Take Jello. The idea was that you would go out and talk to all these women who had recipes where they would use Jello to add their own little special touch to make it extra-special. And you'd end up with a shot of this thing she made, and the husband saying, "hey honey, you are a great cook" and the wife looking at camera and saying, "well, I had a little help," with a wink.

Fortunately, there were a few who did want spots that were funny – intentionally so. Usually small agencies hired by clients with new products or services, they were unimpaired by the mind-sets and bureaucracies of the larger agencies – and willing to take risks. Like Ally Gargano and Federal Express. The success of the Federal Express campaign not only put me on the map but once and for all killed the notion that 'funny' doesn't sell.

There are no 'gags' in my spots. The humour comes from characters who are either trying to keep their cool in a crazy situation, or in denial that

maier

they're even in a crazy situation. The dialogue's pretty banal and always played straight. In auditions, I get irked when asked, "should I play it serious or for comedy?" You always play it serious – that's what makes it funny! (Sellers was brilliant at this. Think of Clouseau, Mandrake, Muffly and all the others.)

Most of the time I use non-professionals – there's no way to build character in 30 seconds. With the non-pro, the character's already there – individual little quirks, tics or habits that they're often unaware of – they haven't learned all the cliché tricks. I know, that might mean seemingly endless takes due to line fluffings or whatever but in the end it's all worth it: the little mistakes or accidents make for a certain magic that I'd never get from a pro.

Early on, I learned I'd never end up with that 'magic' if held down by storyboards or precise scripts. You've got to let a thing grow. After working out the gist of a scene, I don't write the dialogue until after casting, then I write it for that particular actor. Later, during the shoot that actor might say or do something I hadn't thought of, and I'm thinking, "wait a minute, that's a hell of a lot better." Even a 30-second spot can take on a life of its own. Of course you stick with the basic idea, but then let the thing grow – that's what the creative process is all about.

Also, it soon became apparent that the more control I had in that process the better the work. That meant getting involved at the concept stage and following through all the way, up to and including the tape transfer. 'Consultation' over the phone or the idea that you can shoot a thing so that it can only be cut one way is bullshit. I've got to be there; the cut, picking the takes, the voice-over, sound effects, music mix – the end result. It's what ends up on the screen – that's the kick and all that counts.

I've heard people in the business say, "look, it's just a commercial." But I think, whatever takes up your day you damn well better get some satisfaction out of it – or you're just another putz.

Too often technique gets in the way of what's being said. Instead of a means to an end, it becomes an end in itself – and that gets boring after a while. There has to be a reason for everything you do – whenever you move the camera, whenever you make a cut. Form and content are one and the same.

There's also a tendency to ignore or forget that a spot is seen many times over. That's why I like to inject seemingly irrelevant little bits of business – it's the telling of a joke not the punch-line that bears the repetition. For me, style is simply 'point of view'. Those who say they deliberately have no style reveal a lot about themselves.

Valser 'Remote Control'
1992

Client
Valser

Agency
Contexta, Switzerland

Agency Creative
Hannes Weber

Script
Announcer: Owing to the technological advances of Mankind... the quality of life... is constantly changing... for the better.

Pointing and clicking the wrong remote – instead of turning on the TV, he starts the fountain. Attempting to find the right one from the bowl full of remotes he accidentally closes the blinds – triggers the fireplace – and lowers the beds.

Announcer: The quality of Valser never changes. It's been bubbling forth the same refreshing taste... for centuries.

As he relaxes with a tumbler of Valser – his chair collapses.

VALSER.

Fiberglas Canada 'House Named Edna'
1985

Client
Fiberglas Canada

Agency
Goodgall & Associates, Canada

Agency Creative
Trevor Goodgall

Script
Announcer: More than 2 million Canadians have insulated their homes with Fiberglas Pink Home Insulation.

Here's what one particular couple did with the money they saved.

Man: We saved enough for a down payment on what we think is one heck of a lovely summer place.

Man: As you can readily see I named the house after my wife, her name is Edna.

Man: And be that as it may it gives us an opportunity to entertain our many friends from different parts of the country.

Announcer: What you do with the money you save is your business. Our business is making sure you do save money. Fiberglas Pink. Do it for the money you save.

Friend: Bill, old buddy, I think I can speak for all of us in expressing our gratitude and a hearty thank you.

Federal Express 'Fast Talking Man'
1981

Client
Federal Express

Agency
Ally Gargano

Agency Creative
Pat Kelly

Script
Executive: O.K.Eunicetravelplans.IneedtobeinNewYorkonMondayLAonTuesdayNewYorkonWednesdayLAonFriday?Gotit?

Eunice: Gotit!

Executive: Soyouwanttoworkhere?Whatreallymakesyouthinkyoudeserveajobhere?

Job Applicant: WellIthinkonmyfeetI'mgoodwithfiguresandIhaveasharpmind.

Executive: Excellent.CanyoustartMonday?

Job Applicant: Absolutelywithouthesitation.

Executive: Wonderfulwonderfulwonderful.AndinconclusionJimBillLarryDonDickAdolfandTedbusinessisbusinessandasweallknowinordertogetthejobdoneyouhavetodosomethingandinordertodosomethingyouhavetogettoworksolet'sgettowork.

Executive: Peteryoudidabangupjob.I'mputtingyouinchargeofPittsburgh.

Peter: Pittsburgh'sperfect.

Executive: IknowPittsburgh'sperfectPeter.That'swhyIpickedPittsburgh.Pittsburgh'sperfect.CanIcallyouPete?

Peter: CallmePete.

Executive: Pete.

Secretary: There'saMrShnitlerheretoseeyou.

Executive: Tellhimtowait15seconds.

Secretary: Canyouwait15seconds?

Shnitler: I'llwait15seconds.

Executive: CongratulationsonyourdealinDenverDave.I'mputtingyoudownforadealinDallas.DonisitadealDowehaveadeal?It'sadeal.I'vegottodisconnectI'vegotacallcomingin.HiBilljustdoublechecking.DisconnectingDick.DisconnectingDon.DisconnectingDork.

Announcer: In this fast paced, high pressure, get it done yesterday world, aren't you glad there's one company that can keep up with it all? Federal Express, when it absolutely, positively has to be there overnight.

Kay Jewelers 'New Man'
1987

Client
Kay Jewelers

Agency
Lieber Katz, USA

Script
Young salesman's first day on job – being filled in on the finer points of the business. An older salesman is continuously shaking a watch, then holding it up to his ear. The manager paces back and forth adjusting his toupée. The assistant manager is fussing about checking price tags, etc.

Young Man: I think I understood...

Older Salesman: New Man?

Manager: Mmmm.

Young Man: You buy the diamond at 200 dollars, mark it up to 3000 dollars, then discount it to 2000 dollars.

Assistant Manager: Correct. An 1800 dollar profit.

Manager: That's the business.

Young Man: So, you mark it up, you're so far up that when you come down, you're still up.

Manager: Up.

Assistant Manager: Up, that's correct.

Manager: Up, that's the business.

Young Man: Why not mark it up to 4000 dollars?

Manager: Ethics.

Assistant Manager: Correct.

Young Man: Ahhh.

Manager to Older Salesman: They're quartz, Jack.

Announcer: At Kay Jewelers we guarantee the honest value of your diamond for a lifetime – in writing. When you do business at Kay, we don't give you the business.

Tank 'n Bowl 'Ed'
1986

Agency
Barraci, USA

Agency Creatives
Bob Barraci
Jim Copacino

Script
Sound of school bell.

Announcer: The exclusive Ungerford School for boys. Total enrolment, 72.

Ed: Very exclusive. Each boy has his own personal toilet.

Eli: That's a lot of toilets.

Ed: 72.

Eli: A lot of toilets.

Announcer: To clean the 72 toilets, custodian Edin E. Buecher –

Ed: Ed.

Announcer: ...and Eli Himmelstein –

Eli: Eli.

Announcer: ...don't use a brush, a cleanser, or a disinfectant.

Eli: You simply use one of your favourite fingers.

Ed: I use my index finger.

Announcer: You see, every Ungerford toilet has Tank 'n Bowl which automatically cleans, deodorises, and kills germs every time you flush.

Ed: Without scrubbing. And it lasts up to 4 months. (Holds up five fingers).

Eli: Sometimes 6.
(Holds up all 12 fingers)

Announcer: New Tank 'n Bowl. You'll never scrub again. So unique, it's patented.

Ser

Inspired by film-makers such as Truffaut and Fellini, Michael Seresin left his job as a PA at Pacific Films in his native New Zealand in 1961 to pursue a career as a freelance camera assistant in Europe. After eighteen months in Rome and London he had graduated to lighting cameraman status and by 1968 was working alongside his future BFCS partners Bob Brooks and Len Fulford. Seresin began directing in 1972, combining a career as a director of photography on films by Harold Becker, Adrian Lyne and Alan Parker – most notably 'Bugsy Malone', 'Midnight Express' and 'Angel Heart'. He is now considered to be one of the best lighting cameramen in the world, as well as a director with a classic feel for narrative. His commercials credits include Fiat 'Train' , VW 'Casino' , 'Jacques de Florette' for Stella Artois and the long-running 'Nicole' campaign for Renault UK. Seresin co-owns the production company BFCS with director Derek Coutts. He has won over 40 top advertising awards and when not making films his interests include his acclaimed vineyard, Seresin Estate, in New Zealand.

I was first drawn to directing after watching too many French and Italian New Wave films as a student in New Zealand. I think it explains why I've always felt more like a movie person than an advertising person. And why my perspective is different from directors who come from an ad agency background. When I read a script I read it cinematically. And when I shoot I always strive to give cinematically what the concept calls for.

I've worked on twenty features at the last count. I used to shoot films and intersperse them with commercials. Now it's more the case that I shoot commercials and intersperse them with films. One every couple of years or so.

This balance actually helps my directing in both areas. Making a commercial is a phenomenal discipline. It combines and distills all the film-maker's skills. And you have to make it work in the time. I've always got my eye on the stopwatch. In that respect it's much more exacting than shooting a feature.

Features on the other hand satisfy the lighting cameraman in me. A broader canvas. Three- or four-minute shots, moving all over the place. You have to have a different kind of ingenuity to work that out.

My basic attitude to film-making is to capture everything in-camera first, rather than shooting something and thinking I can make it right later. I don't like doing things on the original negative because if you decide you don't like it afterwards, you're stuffed. I can't imagine looking at rushes and still being nowhere near what the final film is going to look like.

Even so, what's happened in post production in the last few years is very exciting. And sometimes you just can't solve everything while you're filming. The De Beers campaign I did a few years back is a case in point. I enjoyed the process enormously.

For me, the best work has a balance, an increasingly elusive combination of idea and look. Style and content. Perhaps because of this preference, most of the work I do focuses on story-telling. Whenever I get a script the first thing I ask is whether I like the story. Is it powerful, interesting, dramatic, fresh? Is it a challenge? Can I contribute anything new?

It's always fascinating to see how your interpretation of a script, which you visualise as you read, changes after talking to the creatives and finding out how they see it. The process of distillation – I have a point of view, you have a point of view – is what this business is all about. I'll pass on a script if I genuinely feel I have nothing to contribute to the idea. You come to know what you're good at.

I think the best directors combine excellent technical skills with a strong intuitive sense. Head and heart, if you like. Not that you can pin everything down. That's the beauty of the job. There's always an element of the unquantifiable. The possibility that you knew it was going to be good, but not that good.

The possibility of a moment's magic.

Michael Seresin

Train　　　　**Casino**

Fiat 'Train'
1980

Intentions to shoot the family saying farewell to their grandmother at a railway station outside Rome were scuppered a few hours before shooting, when the local mayor reneged on his agreement to give the crew access. Instead, the team decamped to a site near Tuscany where the road shots were due to be filmed, and found an alternative station half an hour's drive from the nearest village.

Volkswagen 'Casino'
1986

Having failed to cast the ad in London, the team found their hero in Paris. The commercial was shot in the South of France at dawn and dusk to ensure the right lighting for the spot. The casino in the opening shots is, in fact, a town hall dressed especially for the occasion.

Agency
Collett Dickenson Pearce

Creatives
John O'Driscoll
John Kelly

Producer
Ronnie Holbrook

Agency
Doyle Dane Bernbach

Creatives
Tony Brignull
Rob Morris

Producer
Glynis Sanders

Bulletproof   Early

Pilkington 'Bulletproof'
1987
Scenes of actor Timothy West being shot behind bullet-proof glass were genuine and created at Shepperton Studios. However, to be on the safe side, the gun was not actually fired in the direction of West's head as it seems in the ad. Instead, the marksman shot at an angle from below so that the trajectory of the bullet did not target his body. The whole production, from getting the job to finishing the ad, took about a week.

Piat d'Or 'Early'
1987
Filmed on location in Paris.

Agency
Saatchi & Saatchi

Creatives
Simon Dicketts
Fergus Fleming

Producer
Angie Mickleburgh

Agency
Burkitt Weinreich Bryant Clients

Creatives
Neil Brothwell
Martin Hodges

Producer
Angie Mickleburgh

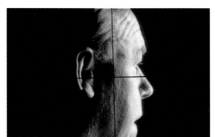

Volkswagen 'Squeak'
1990
Although shot in Southern Spain, all the necessary props were shipped over from Britain, causing a few headaches. The garage was designed and built in the UK by Alan Parker's designer, Brian Morris, but arrived on location badly damaged and needed to be reconstructed on the spot. The snake and other animals seen at the beginning were also brought over with their trainer. Finding long stretches of road that were not lined with fields covered in plastic grow-sheets proved tricky.

Stella Artois 'Jacques de Florette'
1990
Another long-running campaign that I created the original look for. This first ad in the series was shot in Aix en Provence to capture the feel of the film 'Jean de Florette' but used none of the actual locations, which were all deemed unsuitable for the ad. However, the production team did use the same local 'gofer' who had worked on the movie, who, it turned out, had thousands of the original silk carnations from the production under his bed and was able to hire them out at a fee. Scenes of Jacques with his donkey had to be shot on a road with clearly sloping sides. The BACC specified this at script stage because they didn't want any hint that an intoxicated, post-drink Jacques might lose control of the beast, allowing it to run amok. The inference of the visual was meant to be that if the beast did escape, it would only tumble off the road, rather than into a crowd.

Agency
Boase Massimi Pollitt

Agency
Lowe Howard-Spink

Creative
John Webster

Creatives
Charles Inge
Jane Garland

Producer
Michael Hayes

Producer
Michael Hayes

Interesting

Diamond Engagement Ring

Renault Clio 'Interesting'
1991
I cast and created the look for the Papa/Nicole strategy, which has proved an enduring campaign for Renault. This first-ever ad was shot in out-of-season Aix en Provence and required a good deal of set dressing. The local chateau where Papa and Nicole were supposed to live had a drive in need of regravelling and lacked plants, while the ivy crawling up the side of the restaurant (actually a shop) had no leaves and had to be enhanced artificially. The final problem was Nicole herself, who it turned out could not drive and had to be given a crash driving course.

De Beers 'Diamond Engagement Ring'
1992
Producer Michael Hayes and I created a hitherto unused technique to make this famous campaign, of which this is one of the first. It uses motion control camerawork to build up layers of shadows, followed by weeks of post production work to add other details and ensure that everything that should not be seen is blacked out. Tests were originally done at BFCS's own in-house studios before moving to Pinewood.

Agency
Publicis

Creatives
Tago Byers
Mel Williams

Producer
Michael Hayes

Agency
J. Walter Thompson

Creatives
Joanne Mawtus
Anna Moult

Producer
Michael Hayes

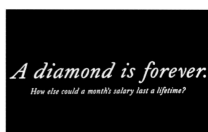

Peter Smillie

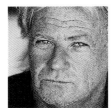

Born in the South African city Durban in 1949, Peter Smillie started out as a photographer before switching to directing at Philo Pieterse Productions in Johannesburg. In 1984 he emigrated to America and began working with Robert Abel & Associates in Hollywood. Two years later he joined Berkofsky/Smillie/Barrett in LA before establishing Smillie Films in 1988. Renowned for his visual innovations and daring cinematography, Smillie has received many international honours, including the prestigious Directors' Guild of America 'Director of the Year' prize in 1991, Adweek's 'Director of the Year' in 1992, the Japan Fuji Sankei Award and numerous Gold Lions at Cannes. In 1993 he was a guest speaker along with Joe Pytka and Ridley Scott at the inauguration of the AICP's 'The Art & Technique of the American Commercial' at the Museum of Modern Art in New York. In 1996 he was voted 'Best Foreign Director' at The Midsummer Awards in London.

What we do pretty much lives and dies by whom we're doing it for. If I don't know the creatives then the script at least has to be original, because 20 million people are going to see it, so it's devastating if it's only some regurgitation of an old idea or established style. I've been doing this for so long now it's boring as hell for me to repeat myself, which happens a lot. This is a very derivative business.

If you go in demanding all the freedom in the world, it's going to be ugly, because to do that you've got to cut everybody out. I know there are some directors who work like that very successfully but shooting commercials is traumatic enough without a war going on.

Making a commercial can be like a clusterfuck: five hundred people sticking their oar in. Sometimes it's very difficult to get something individual out of it. Trying to please too many people means you start playing safe. I guess that's what makes it interesting at the same time – gives it an edge. Every time you make a commercial you're trying to break down these restrictions.

I like collaborating on the concept right up until we shoot. If the agency have a good idea, they came about that by some degree of intelligence so you have to listen: presuming we agree, by the time shooting starts, I expect to be left alone.

I love taking pictures and motivating actors. I actually like the unknown side of film-making, the fact that I don't know what I'm doing. You can prepare as much as you like yet still you're going in blind – and I like that, the whole serendipitous 'whatever happens' kind of thing. I enjoy scaring myself.

I don't beat people up so much. American agencies always used to see me as the Prince of Darkness and only came to me for strange and moody stuff. These days it's something else entirely: comedy dialogue. It was never a conscious decision of mine, so I think agencies just invent reasons why they want you.

I always insist that agencies put the onus on me. I think it's part of my job: I'm there to take a fall, so if they give me half a chance I'll go direct to the client and cajole to get what we want. My clients realise there's a certain consistency to my work and

128

that I can manage pretty much whatever they throw at me from a technical point of view – and do it in a decent manner, with respect for them and the project. I've always had a hard time making a correlation between art and advertising. We're just salesmen basically, flogging commercial art.

I may always do my own cinematography, but I'm not into using bells and whistles to make a commercial my own. I just get bored staring at a monitor bellowing through a megaphone, so I'm prepared to take chances all the time, which professionally DOPs tend not to do.

I figure if the idea is good enough, it will sell the product. If it doesn't, I don't necessarily feel too responsible. I think if everybody goes in there positively – client, agency, director – and it doesn't make an impact on sales then that's just one of those things.

I'm not in this game for the money. A lot of directors shoot fifteen days a month. I don't. Commercials mean you can be very prolific at what you do, so you get enough opportunities to express yourself. I'm not sure there are many other disci-plines – maybe rock music, photography or writing – where there's always a real opportunity to do a lot of what you like doing best – which in my case is putting pictures together, telling stories. I like the nature of commercials. The quick in-out. Some of them are so horrific I would draw a warm bath, get a blunt razor-blade and slit my wrists if they went on any longer!

Are directors overpaid? No way! I think they're worth a lot more actually. It's a huge responsibility to take someone's million dollars and lurch out onto a location somewhere and come back with a good result. Clients are risking a lot on you and I think you should be compensated for it. Competition always makes that happen. It's the same in Hollywood: the competition drives up the price. People will always pay for something better because they have to get something better.

I've worked with pretty much the same crew consistently for twelve years, which means we can short-circuit a lot of problems. We're like a pack of hyenas: if we have somebody new on set, the crew goes round sniffing them out for days. They don't suffer fools gladly. Even if I like the person, if the crew doesn't get on with them, they're out. It's a tribal thing.

I think it's very important that my crew know how I work. If we're getting up at four in the morning to shoot a sunrise with a complicated technical arrangement, they pretty much know which way I'm gonna jump. Having all the toys in line before you start makes it very efficient, which helps a lot in commercials because, pay as much as they like, they never give us enough time to do what we need to do. You're always under the gun, always trying to get more out of the resources you're given.

I'm never satisfied. There's never a perfect commercial. That's what's nice about them and also what's quite ugly about being a commercials director. A journalist once asked me: "If you had to write something on your epitaph in relation to what you do, what would you write?" and I was totally stunned. What I did five years ago, I hate and what I did five weeks ago I kinda like, but that's the nature of commercials.

They come and they definitely go.

Volvo 'Road Ahead'
1997
An opportunity to work with a good friend, Michael Lee at Messner Vetere et al. He's a great creative director who truly understands the maxim "Less is more". In this spot we shot on a half-mile tarmac strip out in the desert. It was a challenge to not repeat oneself too often with the angle and style, but, we pulled off an interesting spot I think.

Henry Weinhard's 'Interview'
1994
A good idea, classic characters with a 90s update. Good casting was paramount as virtually the whole spot takes place on their faces. The nuances of timing and dialogue are what makes it work.

Client
Volvo Cars of North America

Client
G. Heilman Brewing Co.

Production Company
Smillie Films

Production Company
Smillie Films

Director
Peter Smillie

Director
Peter Smillie

Producer
Stephanie Swor

Producer
Stephanie Swor

Advertising Agency
Messner, Vetere, Berger, McNamee
Schmetterer-EuroRSCG/NY

Advertising Agency
The Richards Group/TX

Agency Producer
Christina De Louise

Agency Producer
Jessica Coats

Art Director
Michael Lee

Creative Director
Jim Baldwin

Copywriter
Tony Gomes

Art Director
Mike Renfro

Editor
Roger Harrison @ Cutaways Ltd

Copywriter
Ron Randle

Music
Tom Hadju @ TomandAndy

Editor
Gayle Grant @ Gayle Grant Editing

Visual Effects
Alan Barnet @ Sight Effects

Special Effects
Jim Gill @ Reel Efx Inc

Isuzu 'Body Bag'
1996
A spot with a dark side. Generally black humour appeals to me since the majority of commercials are so soft and 'light'. It was pulled off the air after complaints from the usual suspects came pouring in. Why the industry wastes good money and time listening to this whining bunch of 'politically correct' freaks from the boonies is beyond me.

Peugeot 'Launch'
1995
It was great to get into somebody's head (mainly my own) and put down images that appealed to me in a random but meaningful way. The spot is all about thoughts and dreams, so it fit – we are the dream factory anyway.

Client
American Isuzu Motors Inc

Production Company
Smillie Films

Director
Peter Smillie

Producer
Stephanie Swor

Advertising Agency
Goodby, Silverstein & Partners, San Francisco

Agency Producer
Stacy McClain

Creative Director
Rich Silverstein

Art Director
Todd Grant

Copywriter
Chuck McBride

Editor
Tom Muldoon @ Nomad Editing

Client
Peugeot

Production Company
Smillie Films

Director
Peter Smillie

Producer
Stephanie Swor

Advertising Agency
EURO/RSCG Wnek Gosper, London

Agency Producer
Geoff Stickler

Creative Director
Mark Wnek

Art Director
Nigel Rose

Editor
Roger Harrison @ Cutaways Ltd

Music/Sound Design
Machinehead

MCI 'Road'
1992
Another Michael Lee concept. Anna Paquin, the actor, was 12 years old at the time. She's basically a genius in front of the camera. She went on to win an Oscar for her part in 'The Piano' after we shot the spots.

Labatt's Ice 'Seventh Game'
1994
Another spot that veered into darker territory. Threatening yet humourous. Again, the agency participated a lot by going with the casting and location etc. Any job where you run into obstacles immediately in casting and location, you can kiss goodbye. There's just not that many choices or options out there.

Client
MCI

Production Company
Smillie Films

Director
Peter Smillie

Producer
Stephanie Swor

Advertising Agency
Messner, Vetere, Berger,
McNamee Schmetterer, New York

Agency Producer
Tom Meloth

Art Director
Michael Lee

Copywriter
Paul Wolf

Editor
Roger Harrison @ Cutaways Ltd

Client
Labatt's

Production Company
Smillie Films

Director
Peter Smillie

Producer
Stephanie Swor

Advertising Agency
Ammirati & Puris, Toronto

Agency Producer
Dee Anderson

Creative Directors
Tom Nelson
Doug Robinson

Art Director
Steve Jurisic

Copywriter
Josh Denburg

Editor
Andy Attali @ Chameleon

Citroën 'Bankheist'
1994
The French! I love them! Gilbert Scher, Pascale Petit, J.J. Grimblat, Jean-Marc the client – all very savvy people who see making spots just like I do. It's got to be fun!

Martell '1993'
1993
This shoot was all about image. Great locations (Paris) and good looking people with carte blanche as to what was shot. We had a vague concept of doing something period but not obviously so. In fact, all the wardrobe was Galliano and Dolce & Gabbana. Sort of retro 90s feel. A really fun shoot.

Client
Citroën

Production Company
Smillie Films/Hamster Publicité

Director
Peter Smillie

Producers
Stephanie Swor
Jean-Jacques Grimblat
Herve Lavayssiere

Advertising Agency
Euro RSCG, Paris

Agency Producer
Pascale Petit

Creative Director
Gilbert Scher

Art Director
Stephane Franck

Copywriter
Laurent Dupont

Writer
Jean-Christophe Royer

Editor
Andy Attalai @ Chameleon

Client
Seagram's Martell-Cognac

Production Company
Smillie Films

Director
Peter Smillie

Producer
Stephanie Swor

Advertising Agency
DDB Needham, New York

Agency Producer
Eric Hermann

Creative Directors
Jack Mariucci
Bob Mackall

Editor
Roger Harrison @ Cutaways Ltd

Where does the inspiration for your films come from?

When I was at film school, a guy asked me "What should I read, what should I look at so that I can improve my work?" I told him that was entirely the wrong question. I know it's a cliché, but it's like when Picasso was asked how he dared to charge so much money for a painting that only took 30 minutes. He answered that it actually took him 45 years and 30 minutes.

In other words, there's a lot of yourself invested in your work...

You're paying for a whole life. When an agency sends me a storyboard they're basically paying for me growing up in the Himalayas for ten years, selling cars for five years, living in LA, living in Delhi, living in Europe, seeing all that together. All the paintings that I've seen, all the trash magazines, all the silly books I've found in libraries, all the Tarkovsky movies I've watched... all the porno films at 2 o'clock in the morning.

So how do these various experiences in your life relate to your work?

They are a kind of hotchpotch at the back of my head. When I see a script I don't specifically ask somebody to go out and buy me all the books of any photographer who's ever done flowers. I already know who's done flowers. I've done my research. I store things in my brain for years. I puke and it all comes out. A CD I hear today may be perfect for a commercial I'm doing six years down the line. When I need to, I will instinctively be able to retrieve it.

What attracted you to commercials directing in the first place?

What attracts me is that the camera is involved... and I can use the kinds of toys that if I was in the movies I probably wouldn't even know about. I did some of my best work in school – nine commercials for $6000. They stayed on my reel for five years. I promised myself that I would never be tempted by the money in advertising, that I would stick to good ideas and push the parameters. That's the best way to learn. Advertising is my new school.

What's been the most testing period in your career?

Three years ago I split with my girlfriend, Fatima. It was really hard for me personally because she was my production designer, my guru, my everything. She really taught me every aesthetic sense I have. When we separated, I stumbled about for ten months trying to find confidence in myself. I took on a whole bunch of shitty jobs to figure out that she was irreplaceable. I had to wake up and pay attention to things I never had before. After that, it became easier.

Did you have to reassess the way you work?

The first thing I do now is look at what matters most. I make an emotional graph. The script is going up here and it's going down there. Where are the holes that I can fill? Where are the characters I can put in that the agency has missed? A lot of times agencies say, "no, no, no, this idea is strong enough to hold." The trick is having the confidence and self-respect to stand your ground, to say, "no – you've got to push this aspect more, push this one less."

What aspect of directing commercials do you enjoy most?

The part of the process I find most rewarding is figuring it out – when the script arrives and it's down to me to work out exactly what needs to be done. The first seven minutes is pure. Once the storyboard is completed on any job of mine – except something like Superga – you could have my AD shoot it. It's the prefiguring that's me and the years of experience behind me.

You keep coming back to experience...

That's key. My experience of life gives a different perspective to most of the people around me. A Messiah is not a Messiah in his own backyard. If I'd stayed in India, there would have been another billion of me with the same perspective. But I decided to move on and that's what made me different. Originality is the art of concealing your source. There's no original person anywhere. So where you grew up, who beat you, who buggered you when you were small, what you read, what you did – everything – that's what makes you special.

What qualities do you look for in an actor?

In commercials the role of the performer is really exaggerated. It is nothing. In 95 per cent of commercials we are expected to do professional casting – and even when I see a person who couldn't act their way out of a cupboard I know that they'll be fine by the time the ad has been cut. The format we're dealing with is so small you could make a table act.

And what about your crew?

I grant total freedom to the crew. That's the problem: these guys do not get the credit they deserve. My art directors solve 95 per cent of my problems. My only role is to grasp the overall picture and to remember that the product is sacred, that we're not in show business. If you have found people you trust with the details, do not fuck with them because they will give you the world. Have confidence in them and let them perform.

So where does the director fit into this set-up?

I get all the credit, but I do not believe in auteur this, auteur that. Production is about teamwork and anyone who has worked with me will know that the only person who isn't irreplaceable is me. Anyone

who pretends to be an artiste just bugs the fuck out of me. Every director is surrounded by a network of people helping to make their stuff special.

Is there an underlying style to your work?

My showreel should have a common thread – but should look like it's been done by ten different directors. There's a very focused goal – flexibility. Agencies love to pigeonhole. I'd rather be in a position where they consider me for a script and say, "fuck me, he hasn't done anything like this before so maybe he'll do it." I don't want agencies to be able to focus in on what I like to do.

How did you get your first big break?

At school, the first music video I did was REM's 'Losing My Religion' – and everybody goes, "what a lucky bastard, how did you pull that off?" But if you'd seen my school work up to that point, you'd know REM would have been suckers not to have employed me. The same goes for Levi's 'Swimmer' commercial. And I hope the same will hold true when I do my first movie. I sold cars to pay my way through college. So when I have a good thing to sell I just walk in with my salesman shoes on and say, "give me the fucking job."

Tarsem

Swimmer   Elephant

Levi's 'Swimmer'   Coca-Cola 'Elephant'
1992   1994

Tattoo   India Red/Cricket

Centraal Beheer 'Tattoo'   Coca-Cola 'India Red/Cricket'
1993   1996

Good v Evil   Message in a Bottle

Nike 'Good v Evil'   Smirnoff 'Message in a Bottle'
1996   1993

The Challenge   **Washroom**

Superga 'The Challenge'
1997

Levi's 'Washroom'
1996

Tikho

Based in São Paolo, Brazil, João Daniel Tikhomiroff has been making commercials for 25 years. He is the founder and director of JODAF, one of the top production companies in Latin America. His work has won 36 Lions at the Cannes Festival (including 11 Golds), Gold, Silver and Bronze medals at the New York Television Festival as well as the Grand Prix at the Japan Festival.

My father worked as the general manager of Universal Studios, so when I was a kid, I was always in the projection room, watching films. I went to study at film school in Rio de Janeiro where I made my first shorts. Then, when I was 22 and very crazy, I started to shoot my first feature film. I didn't finish it because I ran out of money. A friend of mine said, "why don't you make a commercial and with the money you receive you can finish off the film." And someone was mad enough to give me that opportunity. That's how I became a commercials director. I never did finish the feature film (it was probably terrible anyway).

I love good ideas. I love to sit with creative teams and help them with the idea and the script. Sometimes it needs something extra. When I did the commercial for Phebo perfume, the idea was of a woman putting the scent on after her bath, watched by her daughter from the door. So I thought, wouldn't it be fantastic if we put them together, and saw the little girl copy everything her mother was doing, like a reflection in the mirror. The commercial went on to run for three years in Brazil.

If the original idea is very strong, you shouldn't mess around with it or you can lose it. It may just need a little touch to make it come to life. I shot a fantastic script for Lego in which you saw what famous people made with their Lego when they were kids, for example Steven Spielberg (a dinosaur) or Mike Tyson (a dismembered boxer) or Pelé (a football). All I added to the idea was the object's shadow moving across the shot to give the images

miroff

some animation. That was all it needed.

I usually do a storyboard and take it back to the team to discuss my approach. I don't have a personal style. If I had only one style to shoot commercials, my career would have lasted two or three years, no longer. And it's boring to shoot everything in the same way. I allow the idea to determine the style.

I also think about what the most important element of the commercial will be. Sometimes it's the casting, sometimes the lighting, sometimes the art direction – sometimes it can be the caption at the end. I don't like video effects, but on one commercial I did for a school, I remembered David Hockney's work with Polaroids, and I thought it would help the aesthetic of the film if we copied this effect in post production.

With casting, I'll give a lot of time to finding the right people – even if it means cutting the amount of time I have for post production. How I direct the actors depends on the actor and the idea. The day before I shoot, I'll meet with them to talk about the film. This helps me to see what kind of personalities they are, how much direction they'll require. Some actors need a lot of time dedicated to them, others need to be left alone. You have to understand the mind of an actor to know his needs.

I have to be involved in the choice of music for a commercial. It helps me to get the mood right. Before I did the perfume film with the mother and daughter, I was listening to an old recording of Billie Holiday at home. When I heard the song, 'I'll Never Be The Same', I got very excited, because I knew I had found the perfect piece for the commercial. I shot it with the music in my mind, and then when I showed the cut to the client with the song, he loved it and they bought the copyright to use it.

You need three things to become a director. The first is talent.

The second is training. Directing is a very difficult, complicated profession so it helps if you absolutely understand the job. For this reason, I would say it is better to go to a good film school, than to try to learn by making pop videos or starting in an advertising agency.

The last thing is perseverance. You won't make the best commercial ever the first time you try. You must always be prepared to improve.

João Daniel Tikhomiroff

Mae e Filha Passeata

Phebo 'Mae e Filha'
1988
A little girl is imitating her mother in a poetic feminine fantasy

Staroup Jeans 'Passeata'
1988
Young people in a student demonstration are stopped by the police. The atmosphere is ironic and humorous, with a voice-over explaining the product.

Script
That's the pleasure of being a woman

Music
Billie Holliday: 'I'll Never Be The Same'

Script
Staroup jeans, the most worn jeans Brazil.

Due to a special washing process, Staroup jeans really look cool.

Staroup are tough and unbeatable.

Staroup passed the most rigourous quality controls. They give total freedom to your movements.

Staroup ... the most tried and tested, the most worn.

If your jeans aren't Staroup, protest

Brahma Bock 'Artisan'
1995
Scenes of a man who cultivates barley and makes his own beer. After a hard day's work, he tries his own brew and realises that it's horrible; he then drinks Brahma Bock and recognises the difference – it's delicious.

Sebrae 'Enfermeira'
1996
A nurse tells babies, as if they were adults, what they are supposed to do about taxes – representing the way government was treating small business.

As a result of this campaign the congress sanctioned a new law giving different taxes and less bureaucracy for small and micro companies.

Text
The bock for the number one beer.

Script
Nurse: Order of the day:
nine am – pay city permit;
eleven am – deduct social security trust;
twelve am – pay fees;
one pm – pay taxes.

Speaker: This is more or less the way Brazil has been treating small business. Legislation that doesn't make sense.

Nurse: Any questions?

Voice-over: It's time to change, so small business will have a chance to grow.

Nurse: I don't hear any crying.

João Daniel Tikhimiroff

Duellists

Famous Children

Muricy 'Duellists'
1994
Two duellists pace away from each other in an atmosphere of suspense. They disappear out of the frame. The sound of shots and a falling body can be heard (but not seen).

Voice-over: Buy a larger TV set. Buy a 32" Sony at Muricy.

Lego 'Famous Children'
1995
This commercial features a range of Lego shapes with moving shadows, including a dinosaur made by Steven Spielberg, aged 5; a series of windows by Bill Gates, aged 5; and a bed by 4 year-old Madonna.

Boulevard Rosa 'Crime'
1997
A commercial for a shopping centre. Police officers are checking a corpse and are disgusted with the clothes the dead person is wearing.

Varig 'Passport'
1997
A customs officer is checking the passports of international passengers on their arrival. As usual, the photos never look like the same person after a long trip. He is amazed when a man who has travelled in Varig's new Executive Class does look the same as his photograph.

Script
Comisario: Let's go

Ayudante: There it is

Comisario: Show me

Woman: Oh my god!

Ayudante: Horrible. Never seen anything like this.

Comisario: Me neither. Look at that shirt and those trousers and those shoes. Dreadful!

Off: Boulvard Rosa. You need it

Ayudante: Cover it up, Jesus, cover it up.

Script
Voice-over: Get there looking the same as you left. Travelling Varig's new Executive Class.

Customs Officer: No

Passenger: What do you mean

Customs Officer: That's not possible!

Voice-over: New Varig's working non-stop to please you.

Born in France to an Italian mother and French father, Kinka Usher was exposed to visual arts, theatre, literature, music and dance while growing up in Europe. After moving to Santa Barbara he pursued his goal to succeed in the entertainment industry by experimenting with film and stills cameras. Eventually he moved to San Francisco and juggled careers as a sous chef and photographer. Three years later he was back in LA, hungry for some involvement in the production business, taking a job as a PA on various commercials and feature films. In 1985 he became a freelance camera assistant. When he first worked with Joe Pytka he realised directing commercials was like coming home. After stints at Stiefel & Co and Smillie Films he founded House of Usher Films in 1996. For two years in succession he has been nominated in the Directors Guild of America Awards. In June 1997 he collected one Gold, one Silver and two Bronze Lions at Cannes for his Polaroid, California Milk, Nissan and Pepsi campaigns – after having 15 commercials on the shortlist.

My bank manager's happy but I have no time to do anything but work. You give up a tremendous amount of your personal life in order to get somewhere like this. There's always this kind of nagging sense that tomorrow it will all change. All you need do is look back into the past. Many directors who were really busy while I was coming up have completely disappeared.

It may be a fickle business, but I really enjoy the intense nature of what we do. The good thing about advertising is that you're dealing with people who move fast, who are always ready to do something special. Within days of the bidding stage you can be off shooting somewhere you'd never expect. I think the spontaneity of working in short bursts is incredibly exciting: not knowing what's happening next month, not having your life planned out, always looking forwards.

I'm known as a story-teller who tends not to get fixated on minor details. The thing that gives me the greatest pleasure is great performances from actors. That's a large responsibility for a director, as is structure – my other strength. My weaknesses are achieving the slick-looking film that directors whom I admire and envy can do. I would love to be able to create film that looked like it was shot by Peter Smillie or Jonathan Glazer. Having said that though, when I look at Michael Bay's and even Tarsem's work, I don't identify with their characters, I don't identify with the humanity that's coming through. I think it looks great, it's amazingly art directed but to me the primary responsibility of the director is characterisation, so that people watching the spot become enamoured with the characters through the performance, through the story. I've really focused and pushed hard toward achieving that.

To me, the most important thing is a well thought-out idea – and I have an in-built instinct for good scripts. Concept is everything.

I am careful not to let my ego get in the way of the brand. The first bridge to build is to work out how the agency see themselves within their scripts.

I then constantly talk to the client about their concerns because agencies aren't always truthful about their intentions.

I always make it clear exactly what we're doing and how the product is being positioned. I'd prefer to be known as an ad man more than a director because to me the responsibility is more than just directing: it's helping the client position their product so that they can be more successful. They invest in advertising for a reason and I think we all have a responsibility to give back to them what they're looking for – and more. Too many directors only focus on what a job can do for them.

In order to be a successful director today you really need to know post production inside out. So many scripts call for compositing and CGI, it's rare to shoot a pure idea. I try to keep post at bay because I'm interested in polishing, not solving all my problems there. I tend to shoot practically. The challenge is figuring out how to make the post less of an influence. I do think though that in order to

be a really well-rounded director you need to be educated, to understand everything about post and maybe never use it – like the way Picasso had the ability to paint a classical painting but never chose to. I think that directors are highly paid because of their skill and the responsibility. When you're doing brand advertising for a client who's got sales in the billions of dollars, that's a huge responsibility both for the agency and the director. But ultimately it's the director who brings the whole idea to life. Doing ads that run all over the world is a colossal responsibility and I don't know how you put a price tag on that.

What I enjoy the most is the actual shooting, because all this effort and energy that everyone's expending is condensed into this single frame – and the control always boils down to the director. That to me is so interesting, so mysterious. And it gives me such a buzz.

The second most pleasurable experience is having this kind of family with me: my crew. They insulate and protect me.

Commercials replace my family, my girlfriend, everything. People think that's unbalanced but in reality I get so much pleasure from so many aspects of the business. I certainly have never been any happier. I still pinch myself at times about all the fun things that I'm able to do and all the great people I work with.

I get called by aspiring directors the whole time and my advice is always the same: don't ever sacrifice yourself; don't ever shoot for the money. Always shoot for the idea. It's so important that you shoot what's right for you. I know that a lot of directors take on things that they shouldn't because they're ill advised by executive producers who have their own vested interests. When you're young, you're so impressionable. Get in with the good creatives, find an agency that creates work that you love and go after that agency. That's what I've done and it's worked incredibly well. If you love Jeff Goodby, if you love Lee Clow – go after those guys, start small and bug them and bug them and bug them.

Kinka Usher

Toys
Toys
Meter Maid

Nissan 'Toys'
1996

Agency
TBWA Chiat/Day, Venice CA

Nissan 'Meter Maid'
1996

Agency
TBWA Chiat/Day, Venice CA

Pepsi 'Club'
1996

Agency
BBDO, New York

Polaroid 'Dog and Cat'
1995

Agency
Goodby Silverstein & Partners, San Francisco

Sega 'Morgue',
1994

Agency
Goodby Silverstein & Partners, San Francisco

Mountain Dew 'Jackie Chan'
1996

Agency
BBDO, New York

Founders Club 'Dave's Putt Putt'
1994

Agency
Stein Robaire Helm

Got Milk? 'Trix'
1995

Agency
Goodby Silverstein & Partners, San Francisco

Got Milk? 'Interrogation'
1995

Agency
Goodby Silverstein & Partners, San Francisco

Vaughan

After 8 years directing music videos (most notably for Simply Red, Terence Trent D'Arby, Soul II Soul, Paul Weller, Jamiroquai and George Michael), Vaughan Arnell and Anthea Benton began to direct commercials in 1991. The success of Wrangler 'DJ' instantly established them. In 1994, Levi's 'Creek' swept the board at awards ceremonies in the UK and Europe. Their partnership continued to thrive until 1996 when they decided to begin directing on their own.

You can't go into this industry without understanding that the basis of everything you're doing is that somebody is selling something to the public – a product, concept, idea, attitude. Yes, you have to make an arresting piece of work that stops people going to put the kettle on in a commercial break, but if afterwards they can't remember what it's for, then you've completely failed.

When we are approached, we always bombard the agency with questions. How did you get to this point? What are you trying to communicate? What do you want people to take from the commercial when they watch it? The greatest compliment we've ever been paid was by the Levi's client who said to us after we'd made Wrangler 'DJ', increasing sales by 20%, "it's the first time we've been scared by a competitor."

Film is definitely the most powerful medium in our world. When you discover a passion for it, nothing else comes close. We started in music videos, and continued doing them until we'd explored every technical aspect of film-making. That meant that

when we moved into commercials, there was nothing anybody could throw at us that we couldn't handle. Making films is like painting – if you don't know how to draw, ultimately you're never going to be able to paint. If the idea is good on paper, then we have the expertise to deliver it – perfected and polished to the nth degree – on film. We've never tried to cultivate a personal style – being pigeon-holed has always seemed to us like the kiss of death. We try to bring a unique approach to everything we do. We never imitate ourselves.

Some scripts come in and they're brilliant; you want to go out and shoot them immediately. Sometimes they need another dimension. Smirnoff 'Wedding' was originally set in a contemporary restaurant. By making it a slightly period Russian wedding, we gave the idea a stronger context in which the story and imagery could unfold. Other scripts are more complicated – somebody's had a conceptual idea which isn't earthed in visuals at all. Then you have to sit there and work out how you're going to to represent the idea visually. If something

& Anthea

isn't right for us, we say no. There are times when you wish you owned the bloody agency because you know the idea ain't good enough, and you want to say, "go home and do better."

As a director, you're trying to encapsulate an idea so that from the first image people can go, "ah, this is what I'm looking at," and be pulled into it. It's up to you to come up with the solution that makes a piece of work gel and gives it a point of view. To do that, you have to put yourself in the situation. You have to research every detail and imagine every possibility. If we were Bonnie and Clyde, how would we walk into the bank we were about to rob? (Entemann's 'Bonnie and Clyde'). What would we want if we had a house in the future? Wouldn't it be brilliant if we had a goldfish tank with no glass in it (Levi's 'Planet'). That's how everything starts.

We never present people with written ideas of what we're going to do. We go into a suite and sit down in front of a video camera and describe our concept with a degree of human passion that you could never get on a piece of paper. We also do a

presentation package with pictures so that people can get a sense of the atmosphere. The best things we've shot aren't storyboarded. Storyboards can be like blinkers; you'll be on set, struggling to do the two-shot you drew and you'll miss the brilliant wide that's begging to be seen.

As a partnership, we had to make sure that we could describe everything we wanted to do with one voice. When we went into the pre-production meeting or walked onto a set, we'd have discussed every aspect of the film. We'd have argued all the pros and cons. We'd have fought all our battles in private. That enabled us to work together in pure stereo. Neither of us ever expected to work in a partnership and we're both strong personalities, so we had to learn to compromise.

But we have an uncanny synergy and a lot of respect for each other and that helped us to arrive at the same point even though we may have started from differing points of view. We spent thirteen years effectively being one person. The most difficult thing about beginning to work apart has been remember-

ing to say 'I' instead of 'we'.

When we started in commercials, there was this group of 25 British advertising actors who did everything. People were surprised at the extremes we'd go to get the casting right.

Likewise, you always got the same group of designers and wardrobe mistresses. So you always got the same look. We tried to bring together other influences like fashion and music, and work with people who had real creative talent. If we found someone doing amazing sculpture or making fabulous hats, we'd try to include them in our team. We went out and found bands or DJs to work with us on the soundtrack. That meant the work we did could have a real connection with what was going on in the outside world.

Directors need to expose themselves to more than just what they do and not just say, "yeah, I know the formula which will make this work." You need to experiment — at the end of the day, it's better to have an interesting failure on your hands than a totally boring success.

Wrangler 'DJ'
1994

Entemann's 'Bonnie & Clyde'
1996

Agency
Simons Palmer Clemmow Johnson

Agency
J. Walter Thompson

Art Director
Mark Denton

Art Director
Ken Grimshaw

Copywriter
Chris Palmer

Copywriter
John Donnelly

Creek　　　　　　　　　　　**Les Nouvelles Chaussures**

Levi's 'Creek'　　　　　　　Stella Artois 'Les Nouvelles Chaussures'
1994　　　　　　　　　　　1996

Agency　　　　　　　　　**Agency**
Bartle Bogle Hegarty　　　　Lowe Howard-Spink

Art Director　　　　　　**Art Director**
John Gorse　　　　　　　　Vince Squibb

Copywriter　　　　　　　**Copywriter**
Nick Worthington　　　　　Paul Silburn

155

Smirnoff 'Reflections'
1995

Agency
Lowe Howard-Spink

Art Director
Vince Squibb

Copywriter
Derek Apps

Levi's 'Planet'
1995

Agency
Bartle Bogle Hegarty

Art Director
Andrew Smart

Copywriter
Roger Beckett

Wei

Paul Weiland joined Collett Dickenson Pearce as a copywriter in 1973, working on seminal accounts like Parker Pens, Fiat Strada, Silk Cut and Hamlet. In 1979 he switched to directing at The Alan Parker Film Company. When Parker left for Hollywood a year later, Paul inherited the business, changing the name to The Paul Weiland Film Company. Seventeen years later, the company is firmly established as Britain's leading commercials production house, representing eleven directors. It is ranked second in the world, behind Pytka in California and has been ever-present in the Palme D'Or table at the Cannes Advertising Festival. In 1990 Weiland was voted Britain's 'Commercials Director of the Decade' in *Campaign* magazine's Top 100 league table. In 1993 he won the Chairman's Award for his outstanding contribution to the industry at the British Television Awards, where The Paul Weiland Film Company has been voted 'Production Company of the Year' four years running. As well as directing various award-winning children's dramas for Jim Henson Productions and the world-famous TV series 'Mr Bean', Weiland shot the feature films 'City Slickers II' and 'Roseanna's Grave'.

Commercials are a joke. The best ones that is. Humour definitely sells – which is probably why I'm still here! I like to deal with something that's got a heart, a touch of humour: where one can develop an idea and hopefully add a voice that improves on the original script.

The more experienced you are, the more freedom you demand. There is no point in harnessing someone's talent if you don't expect them to come to life on the script's behalf. I can't work out agencies who hire directors with a track record and then tell them what to do. Where's the chemistry in that? I come from an advertising background so I'm hardly going to sell the product down the river. I've always said that the product is the hero, that the product should be the heart of the commercial and everything should pump from that.

Advertising has been the major part of my life since I was 17. I like the intensity and the transience of commercials. You constantly move on to something new. When you're involved in a film, you live with it for a year yet shooting a commercial is like sitting an exam and getting the results immediately.

I like to think I have a touch of the common man. I've done enough comedy to know what people respond to. My whole career has been built on humour, and you don't stop being funny. I think that ads rightly deserve to be seen as pieces of entertainment – and, like songs, need to be able to stand the test of time because they are seen so many times.

However, I don't entirely agree with the 'commercial as art' argument. It always amazes me that there is an abundance of talent in the visual area, whereas there's only a few people who can actually tell a story well enough to hold people's interest. To be precise is incredibly important – but it's also

and

incredibly difficult. To have a beginning, a middle and an end in 30 seconds is not an easy feat.

I don't subscribe to the school of the storyboard though, nor do I believe in researching or discussing everything to death. I'm into spontaneity, the chemistry between the director and the actor, the director and the situation, the director and a prop. A lot of people have a fear of creating something from nothing – I actually work better when I'm in that vulnerable position where suddenly, from nowhere, my ideas come. If I try to sit down and work out what I'm going to do too much beforehand it takes the spontaneity away – and that comes across in the final film.

I'm a free and analytical person. I love people-watching, so I'm very astute when it comes to casting. The chemistry between director and actors is crucial in commercials. Because of the short nature of ads, actors don't really have time to get into a part. It's

often about someone looking right, reacting more than acting. As a director, the secret is to make an actor feel relaxed and confident, to place their trust in you. Directing is all about pushing. You just have to keep going at people because a good performance is the enemy of a great performance. You learn to know when your moments are.

Collaboration is very important – but within limits. Committees and creativity don't go. It's a cliché, but every ship needs a captain, one voice above the rest.

You're the centre of attention. People are always looking at you to make the decisions so you learn very quickly never to be indecisive. The minute you're indecisive you're face down in the water because everyone wants to be a director and everyone has an opinion. You have to make sure you avoid the chipping in process. Co-operation is one thing,

allowing people to foist their ambitions on you spells trouble. It's a very fine line – like being everyone's analyst and trying not to blow your own top yourself.

Technology in film-making is brilliant. Everything is possible, but there's no point in being different for the sake of it. If the idea needs technology, then fantastic, but when the technology has no idea, you're in big trouble. It's made life very easy for some members of the creative community because they don't necessarily need to use their brains anymore. They can jazz weak concepts up by hiring some wizz-bang director to perfume the pig. Visually-dominant ads may look good, but scratch the surface and there's nothing there. The perfect commercial should be like the perfect film: after you've seen it stays with you, it makes you talk about it, it becomes something that you look forward to seeing again. And again. And again. And again.

Comic Relief 'Red Nose Day'
1991
I wrote and directed this ad in about four hours. It won a Silver at D&AD. See what happens when you don't try!

Heineken 'Lip Sync'
1988
It took weeks of rehearsals for the actors to master the technique of talking out of sync. It was only years later that I discovered that by retarding the soundtrack 15 frames I could have achieved the same effect. Silly Billy.

Sainsbury's 'Romance'
1995
I'd always wanted to do a decent Tampax commercial.
I'd like to thank David Sainsbury for giving me the
opportunity.

Fosters 'Haägen-Dazs'
1992
Two commercials for the price of one. It took a brave
Fosters' client to allow 50 of their 60-second ad to
feature someone else's product. It took a brave
Haägen-Dazs client to allow his product to be
portrayed in such a sexual way. Unbeknown to our
Haägen-Dazs client, the big chiefs above had only
that morning agreed to drop the sexy image, and go
for more family values. And he was promptly fired.

The Guardian 'Point of View'
1986
This intelligent 30-second commercial is probably why since 1987 it's been impossible to win a Gold for advertising at D&AD. It only won a Silver!

Heineken 'Water in Majorca'
1985
The rights to use "The Rain In Spain Stays Mainly On The Plain" would have cost the Heineken client £100,000. Thank goodness they couldn't afford to pay it!

Fire Prevention 'Tank'
1986
An innocent five year-old child walking dream-like
in a burning room. She is being stalked by a 50 ton
Sherman tank spewing flames from its turret. You try
casting that one!

Schweppes 'Strange Taste'
1991
I was very pleased with the way this turned out.
I particularly enjoyed working with the lizard. Colin,
I think his name was.

Roger Woodburn was born in South East London in August 1936. Four years later he moved to the North West when his father Harold was appointed as political cartoonist for the *Manchester Evening News*. After graduating as a graphic designer from the city's Regional College of Art in 1958 he was taken on by director Gerry Anderson at AP Films as a model maker and later a special effects supervisor. In 1965 he set up a sfx unit, Valley Films with lighting cameramen Frank Tidy and Peter Biziou. After working frequently as a second unit director for Ridley Scott, he was persuaded to join RSA Films as a director in 1971. Two years later he founded Park Village with director Peter Webb and producer Mike Stones. In 1995 he was awarded the BTA Lifetime's Achievement Award.

What do I look for in a script? Well, whether the agency have put in the length at the top or left it blank. A really good idea that is original and simple. An awful lot of scripts are rubbish, but often even the good ones are over-written. There are very few scripts these days that have one classic, simple idea. They are not fashionable. Ads have become an orgy of graphic tricks because the new electronic gismos offer so many options. The art department can't bear to have nothing happening. Even documentaries have become a big event, with layers and layers of layers. Often you shoot a classic idea that is very simple, but in commercials it generally gets embellished. This seems to me to be covering up some basic inadequacy in the original idea.

There is a dearth of good copywriting at the moment, but I don't feel its the writers' fault. They are manacled in all directions. It is a combination of several things. The video revolution for a start and the dominance of graphics. Silence is something that you have got to write down in the scripts: the pause,

the comic timing. I work mainly with comedy, but nowadays it can't be verbal because most ads have to run worldwide. Copywriting is a dying art, unless you do it in Esperanto.

All the nuances are disappearing from commercials. Once upon a time, when I was a technician, commercials were aimed at Scotland, or the North or South of England and the subtleties between them were very important. Now the globalisation of products means that an ad has to knock 'em dead in Guatemala as well.

The trouble with big American multi-nationals taking over the world, is that American advertising is squeaky clean. Often the people who make the final decisions about the ads which run here, are sitting in St Louis or Memphis judging these things by their standards – so you end up with a bland ad which is trying to be all things to all men.

I don't work the way some other directors do by throwing my weight around. I prefer the softly, softly approach to get my way. But this does require

dburn

an enormous amount of patience. I am sure the creative team are sussing me out as well – working out whether I think I have a chance in hell of changing their script. And then, of course, you acquire all the other flak: not their problems, but their client's. The agency often use a director as a tool to get an idea through. Even as late as the pre-production meeting, the client may be unsure of the concept and be unable to visualise the finished film, so you are pushed forward as a sort of act, because no one has got the balls to tell them that their stipulations may ruin the idea.

I have never had anything to do with cigarette advertising – even back in the dark ages. My father died of lung cancer and I just sat and watched him smoke himself to death. What a waste. It is one of the things in my life that I feel very strongly about. I have never acknowledged it in the past, but I am slightly concerned that I contributed to the popularisation of Britain's beer culture. Throughout the eighties I worked on most beer accounts. The irony

is I don't drink beer at all and I can never understand what beer drinking has to do with machismo.

I like the in and out nature of commercials. I like the intensity. However, engineering is my other life. I am a closet engineer. Every now and then I need the certainty and reassurance of precision to counterbalance the chaos and craziness of the advertising world. I need to be with boffins. After all, it's boffins who make the world go round.

I hate squeezing jobs in. When I was a freelance technician, I used to look at the director and try to analyse what was going on in his head. On one particular occasion we were all standing by with cameras ready, and clients present, when the director came on set and said, "what is it we are doing to day?" I thought if that ever happens to me, it's time to quit.

Years ago I went to Morocco to shoot. We came back with a commercial, but only just! Every frame was chiselled out of solid granite. There was a military coup, we all had dysentery, our passports were taken away, the equipment was confiscated, and we were

involved in a car accident in which two locals were killed. It affected my attitude. Since then, I think long and hard before choosing to shoot on location!

I like the actual shooting, because it is always a relief to get going after the mind games. But shooting can be physically exhausting. You are constantly trying to keep one jump ahead of the crew. I also love the peace and tranquillity of editing (provided the phones are off the hook), creating a story and an atmosphere. I think editing is at least 25% of the creativity, sometimes as much as 50%.

I have always tried not to get typecast. It has happened – comedy transcends all age groups, market layers and nationalities. I have had a couple of times when creatives have said, "nice to meet you. Right, we need some tricks, what have you got?" The creatives probably spent the whole day staring at a blank layout pad and an empty word-processor screen. But how can you start a meeting like that, putting the cart before the horse? Directors are facilitators. We are not magicians.

Dunlop 'Corporate'
1976
I chose this because it really launched my career, and my subsequent success as a director. I'd been directing before then, but with little recognition. With this film I won my first major awards. When it first came out, it was quite revolutionary both in terms of special effects and advertising content. The film was one of the first corporate commercials covering a wide range of products. It was a rediscovery of slapstick comedy which, as far as I can remember hadn't been used a great deal in advertising. For several years following its airing it was much imitated. Many thanks to Andrew Rutherford.

Agency
Saatchi & Saatchi

Sony 'Lifespan'
1984
A wonderful example of the 'less is better' style of advertising of which there is a distinct dearth at present. It has John Webster's stamp all over it. Written and cut to a music track found by John. No dialogue, no voice-over, classic advertising. Many thanks to John Webster and Sony for being brave enough to allow us to show only the back of the TV.

Agency
BMP

BMW 5 Series 'Birth of a Notion'
1988

The idea for this film came from two directions. The agency had seen the film 'Christine' and had the idea of a car creating itself. I had always been fascinated with the idea of photographing a black car in a black studio and ironically had done some lighting tests of my own. Both these sources came together to produce the film. Some money for further tests was produced, which convinced a somewhat sceptical client that a minimalist view in the darkness of his new 5 Series would work. Technically, it was fairly innovative, as it was all done pre-morph, using a variety of techniques, including time-lapse, moving lights, vacuum forming and by today's standards, very simple video effects. The music by Trevor 'Angel Heart' Jones created tension which seemed to pull all the special effects together. Many thanks to Alfredo Marcantonio, Paul Garrett and BMW for leaving all the parts behind.

Agency
WCRS

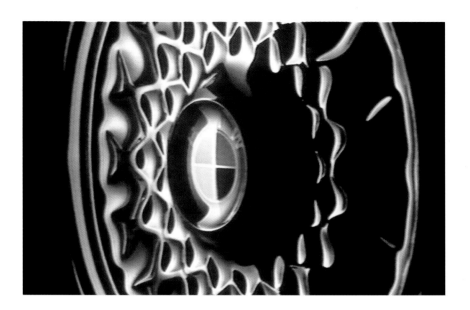

Lee Jeans 'Iron Man'
1993

One of a whole series of Lee Jeans films, which I shot for Fallon McElligott, USA. I'm particularly pleased with this one because it is a one-take commercial. I was interested to see whether I could create the comedy in real time, without the security of covering shots and close-ups. When you shoot a film in one take without close-ups and cutaways, there is no hiding place. You are forced to rely upon casting and performance. As I had a reputation for tricks this film was a test for me, hence I include it here. Many thanks to Mike Lescarbeau and all at Fallon McElligott.

Agency
Fallon McElligott, Minneapolis

Roger Woodburn

Dambusters   **The Incredible Journey**

Carling Black Label 'Dambusters'
1989
Probably the most successful commercial I have made to date and got me the elusive Black Pencil. The film's popularity still seems to endure, even with those beyond the advertising world. Its creation was unique because the air-date was fairly distant. There was very little pressure during the shoot which enabled us to experiment and test all the ideas which would not have been possible under normal scheduling. Because it was for cinema only, and because at that time, video to film transfer quality was appalling, we had to resurrect some old film-based effects; such as front projection, sheets of glass, optical printers, fine grains, inter-positives, inter-negatives, gravity, and of course salt. Many thanks to Jonathan Greenhalgh and Kes Grey.

Heineken 'The Incredible Journey'
1992
I fell in love with the original script, and despite the job going away and returning several times, I was determined to shoot it one way or another. The agency were having great difficulties persuading the client that the idea was a good one. In the end it was shot with a small unit over a long period of time, which enabled us to keep costs down and shooting was very flexible. The agency creatives, Don Barclay, Kevin Kneale and Mr. Patch, doubled up as technicians, and I recommend them to any unit.

Agency
WCRS

Agency
Lowe Howard-Spink

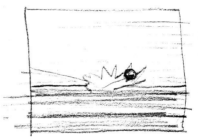   

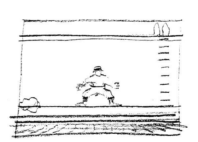   

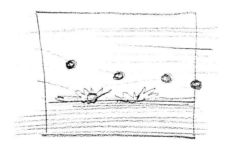   

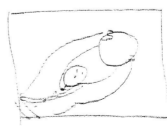   

Abilene   ## Lifeboat

Centraal Beheer 'Abilene'
1994
I included this because I think every director secretly wants to shoot a 'Western'. Erik and Lode were probably the most laid-back, relaxed and self-sufficient creatives I have ever worked with. This, together with the sunshine, had a very positive effect on the film. The music gilded the lily. Many thanks to Erik Wunsch, Lode Schaeffer and Karen Smit.

Alka Seltzer 'Lifeboat'
1997
My most recent success. In an age of complicated, over-written commercials, it was a joy to find an idea of classic simplicity, that harks back to the Sony 'Lifespan' days. It required no embellishment. It was interesting to see how the ITVA coped with cannibalism. Shooting off a dinghy in the Channel is never easy and this was no exception. Both the actors and some of the crew suffered. My gratitude goes to Mike Parker, without whose camera-operating the film would have been unwatchable. Many thanks to Pat Doherty, Greg Marktin and Carol Powell.

Agency
DDB Amsterdam

Agency
Abbott Mead Vickers.BBDO

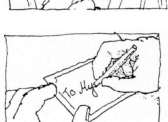   

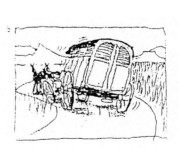   

After serving as a staff photographer in the US Navy and studying at the Los Angeles Art Center, Howard Zieff went on to become one of Madison Avenue's best-known photographers. He began directing commercials in the early 60s. Among many classics are his acclaimed comedies for TWA, American Motors, Benson & Hedges, Volkswagen, Mobil and the legendary Alka Seltzer 'Spicy Meatball'. Dubbed by *Time* magazine as 'Master of the Mini Ha Ha', he extended his comic gifts in a successful feature film-career from 1973, directing comedies such as 'Hearts of the West' starring Jeff Bridges, 'Private Benjamin' with Goldie Hawn and, most recently, 'My Girl' with Macauley Culkin and Jamie Lee Curtis.

I've always enjoyed comedy. Growing up, Frank Capra and Billy Wilder were my heroes. In the Navy, I was sent to the motion picture school. While everybody else was filming trees and birds, I made a three-minute comedy about the life of a cadet. When I subsequently became a photographer, most of my shots were humorous, pseudo slices of life. I decided I could bring the same feeling to commercials. At that time, commercials featured straight-laced WASPs with bright white teeth holding up a package. There was no dialogue, just a voice-over. I was lucky enough to be working with a group of young art directors and copywriters from three or four agencies that were trying to break the mould and stretch the boundaries of what could be done with commercials – see just how far we could go before the client said, "hey, wait a minute, what are you doing?" At first, they were confused and angered by the new approach, but when we eventually became accepted, everybody was asking, "why can't we have one like that?"

What we were trying to do was put real characters in comic situations. We were able to work with some of the terrifically talented young Italian and Jewish actors in New York, kids who were just hanging around looking for a job. That's how I got to cast people like Robert De Niro and Richard Dreyfuss, who were unknowns at the time.

How would I define my style? I enjoy simple concepts that aren't too obvious and don't go too far over the top. I like situations which set themselves up naturally; I cringe when I see characters who are in effect saying, "look at us, we're being funny."

When I began directing, my background in photography made me think I could have a lot of fun with the lighting in commercials. However, I quickly began to realise that's not what the medium is about. I backed off the photographic aspect so I

could focus on the performances. I began going to acting school late nights to understand how to work with actors. I hung out on movie shoots in New York. I remember going up to one actor, after the director gave him five minutes of intense conversation, and saying to him, "I'm trying to understand how to work with actors. What exactly did that director just ask you to do?" "He's so full of shit," the actor replied.

So much for magic words from my gods. I was shocked, because I was an admirer of the director's work, but what it made me realise is that a director isn't there to teach an actor how to act. I learned that when actors show up on set, they're going to give you special gifts – if you let them. They're going to do things you couldn't possibly do. So my technique of delivering direction is not to do too much. If you over-direct, you'll get back a mirror-image of yourself. I want the actor to surprise me, so I'll

describe the scene to him, I'll tell him what the goal is – but not how to reach the goal. I'll never say, this is how I want you to do it. I let him do exactly as he feels, and after the take I tell him if I think he's done something wrong.

I always rehearse for a day before the shoot. I encourage actors to improvise. Very often, they might come up with better lines than the agency. We pay them for their contributions and put them in the script. When we did Hebrew 'Homecoming', the actor playing the uncle sat down at the family piano and began improvising this wonderful Jewish song. We managed to get the rights to it overnight before the shoot, and it made the commercial.

I love detail. When I was in art school, I was a great fan of Norman Rockwell. What I liked in his work were all the little props he used to define his characters and their environments. That stayed with me, and when I began directing commercials, I

always finished dressing the set myself. I'd spend time walking around the space, thinking about what I could put into it. By the time we'd start to shoot, I'd created a whole little world which the actors could inhabit. That's all you need. My frames are very static. I set up a basic tableau and then move the actors around within it.

I always shoot a lot of takes – usually around ten to fifteen. First I go for what I think I want, and then I'll begin to experiment with other ways of doing it.

When I shot my first feature, James Caan said to me, "you got it on the first take. Why are we doing another?"

A couple of weeks later, he was asking me, "can we do another take?" He had begun to enjoy playing with the thing. I love seeing how much further an idea can be carried. There's always more than one solution to a problem.

Howard Zieff

Stomachs **Cashier**

Alka-Seltzer 'Stomachs'
1965

Whirlpool 'Cashier'
1968

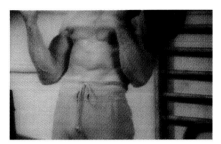

Agency
Jack Tinker & Partners, NY

Agency
Doyle Dane Bernbach, NY

Talent
George Irving
Joe Sirola

172

Talon Zipper 'Great Oculo'
1969

American Motors 'Homecoming'
1969

Talent
Joe Sirola

Agency
Wells Rich Greene, NY

Talent
Robert De Niro
Lou Zorich

Howard Zieff

Clark Candies 'Stolen Goodies'
1967

American Motors 'Driving School'
1970

Agency
Doyle Dane Bernbach, NY

Agency
Wells Rich Greene, NY

Art Director
Stan Dragoti

Writer
Charlie Moss

Talent
Jack Somack
Jane Hallaren
Mark Gordon

Funeral   **Spicy Meatball**

Volkswagen 'Funeral'
1969

Alka-Seltzer 'Spicy Meatball'
1970

Agency
Doyle Dane Bernbach, NY

Agency
Doyle Dane Bernbach, NY

Art Director
Roy Grace

Writer
John Noble

Talent
Jack Somack
Ronnie Graham
Dick Clark (VO)

British Design & Art Direction (D&AD) is a professional association and charity working on behalf of the advertising and design communities. It was formed in 1962 to establish and support standards of creative excellence in the business arena as well as to educate and inspire the next creative generation.

D&AD's activities include the largest and most internationally respected awards scheme in the industry, familiarly known as the 'Yellow Pencils', which attracts over 14,000 entries from around the world each year. Associated with the Awards is the D&AD Annual which sells 13,000 copies and provides the basis of an exhibition which travels the world.

High priority is given to education with a programme of initiatives focusing on students and tutors of design and advertising. The Student Awards, since their initiation in 1979, have formed the centrepiece of the programme, attracting over 1,500 entries from colleges across Europe. Winners of the Student Awards not only have their work showcased in the Student Annual (launched in 1997) but many will also see their work go into production. D&AD's college membership scheme is highly regarded for its excellent resources and Student Expo provides member colleges with the opportunity to show their best work to prospective employers. Particularly popular are the quarterly advertising workshops and the recently re-launched design workshops which attract hundreds of applicants for 20 places.

Successful candidates are invited the meet and work with creative teams from leading agencies and design consultancies.

The President's Lecture series is open to everyone and has proved to be enormously successful. Some of the most respected creative people in the world have spoken, including Oliviero Toscani, Saul Bass, Dave Stewart, Duane Michals, Peter Greenaway, Alan Fletcher and Jeanloup Sieff.

D&AD is supported by individuals and companies and has a membership of 1,600 leading professionals.

For further information please contact

D&AD
9 Graphite Square
Vauxhall Walk
London SE11 5EE
Tel: +44 171 582 6487
Fax: +44 171 582 7784
http://www.dandad.org